Teacher and Ideal Knowledge

Teacher and Ideal Knowledge

Dr. G. Visvanathan
Professor, Department of Education,
Annamalai University, TN
and
Dr. S. K. Panneer Selvam
Assistant Professor, Department of Education
Bharathidasan University, T.N

RANDOM
RANDOM PUBLICATIONS
NEW DELHI (INDIA)

Teacher and Ideal Knowledge

ISBN 978-93-5111-538-0

Published in 2015 in India by
RANDOM PUBLICATIONS
4376-A/4B, Gali Murari Lal, Ansari Road
New Delhi-110 002
Phone : +9111-43580356, 011-43142548, 011-23289044
e-mail : sales@randompublications.com
info@randompublications.com
randomexports@gmail.com

Reprinted 2026

Type Setting by : Shah Computer Graphics, Delhi-110094

Contents

1

Revitalization of Science Teacher Education **1**

Introduction 1
Problems in Science Teacher Education 2
Problems in Selection of the Candidates 3
Poor Knowledge in Preparing Lesson Plans 3
Lack of Knowledge in Preparing and Handling Teaching Aids 4
Problems in Supervision during Practice Teaching 4
Suggestions to Improve Science Teacher Education 4
Conclusion 5
References 6

2

Innovation in Teaching - Learning Process **7**

Modern media and education 8
Web- based learning: 9
Principles of web-based learning 9
e-Learning 10
Advantages of e-learning 10
e-tutoring 10
Computer Assisted instruction (CAI) 11
Merits of Computer Assisted Instruction 11

Computer Managed Learning (CML) 12
Tele-Conferencing 13
Virtual- Education 13
Instruction Modes for Virtual Education 14
Advantages of virtual education 15
Conclusion 15
References 16

3

Flipped Classrooms Learning **17**

Introduction 17
Flipped classroom education 18
What Does a Flipped Classroom Look Like? 18
Flipped Classroom Model 18
Here's how it works 19
Benefits of flipped classroom 19
Administrator role in implementing flipped learning 20
Advantage of flipped classroom learning 21
Disadvantage of flipped classroom learning 22
Conclusion 23
References 23

4

Role of ICT in Educational Transactions **25**

Introduction 25
Utilization of EDUSAT in Schools of Tamil Nadu 27
SITE and its Uses 28
CAI 30
Video Conferencing 30
Virtual Classroom 31
SITE 32
INSAT 32
EDUSAT 32
UGC Country wide Classroom 32
Class Project 33
Learning without Frontiers" (LWF) 33
Conclusion 33
References 34

5

Quality Enhancement in Teaching - Learning **37**

Introduction 37
Develop a Personal Learning Network on Twitter 38
Keep Students Engaged 38
Keep Yourself Organized 38
Communicate with e-mail and Blogs 38
Incorporate a Digital Projector into your Lessons 39
Conclusion 39
References 39

6

Use of ICT For Teaching Psychology **41**

Introduction 41
ICT as a Learning Process 42
ICT- as an Administrative Tool 44
ICT as a Subject 44
ICT as a Medium of Knowledge Management 45
Conclusion 45

7

Traditional Classroom Vs Flipped Classroom **47**

Introduction 47
Flipped Classroom 49
Traditional Vs Flipped Teaching 49
Significance of Flipped Classroom 50
How Does It Work? 50
Implications on Teaching and Learning 51
Key Elements of the Flipped Classroom 51
Steps in Flipping the Classroom 52
Advantages 52
Conclusion 53
References 53

8

Preparing the Academy of Today Learner 55

Introduction 55
Generations and Technology 56
Emerging Patterns 58
Assessing the Generations in Online Learning 59
Excellent Teaching 60
Conclusion 61
References 62

9

Effectiveness of Edu-digital Skill Among Higher Secondary Students 63

Introduction 63
Review of Literature 67
Objectives 69
Methodology 69
Population 70
Attitude Scale Towards Multimedia Programme 70
Scoring 70
Data Collection 71
Hypothesis 71
Administration of retention test 71
Analysis and Interpretation 71
Conclusion 73
References 74

10

Integrating ICT in Education 77

Introduction 77
Use of ICT in Teaching Learning 78
Use of ICT in Diagnostic Testing and Remedial Teaching 79
Use of ICT in Evaluation 79
Use f ICT in Psychological Testing 80
Use of ICT in Developing Virtual Laboratory 80
Use of ICT in Online Tutoring 80

Use of ICT in Developing Instructional Material 80
Barriers of Integration of ICT in Education 81
Teacher Level Barriers 81
School Level Barriers 81
Government commitment to the use of ICT in schools in india 82
Barriers in the Process of Preparing the Teachers 82
Recommendations in the Integrating the ICT in education 82
Conclusion 83

11

Blended Learning Programs 85

Introduction 85
Flex model 87
A La Carte model (formerly Self-Blend model) 88
Enriched Virtual model 88
Conclusion 88
References 89

12

The Impact of Science and Technology Among Students 91

Introduction 91
Digital skill in website 92
Review of Literature 92
Objectives 100
Methodology 100
Sample 100
Data Collection 100
Analysis and Interpretation 100
Gender and attitude towards the use of new technology 100
Null Hypothesis No. 1. 100
Qualification and attitude towards the use of new technology 101
Null Hypothesis No. 2 101
Locality of the School and attitude towards the use of new technology 102
Null Hypothesis No. 3 102
Type of School and attitude towards the use of new technology 102
Null Hypothesis No. 4 102
Level of teaching and attitude towards the use of new technology 103
Null Hypothesis No. 5 103

Teaching Experience and attitude towards the use of new technology 104
Null Hypothesis No. 6 104
Correlation Analysis 105
Correlation Analysis between teachers attitude towards the use of new technology and interest in teaching 105
Null hypothesis No. 8 106
Suggestions 106
Conclusion 107
References 107

13

An Assessment of Edu Digital Skills **111**

Introduction 111
Educational Digital Skills 112
Technological Literacy 113
Information Literacy 113
Global Awareness 114
Objectives of the Study 114
Research Question 114
Research Methodology 115
Population, Sample and Sampling Technique of the Study 115
Tools and Technique of Data Collection 115
Scoring Procedure & Statistical Tools Used 116
Educational Implications 120
Conclusion 120
References 120

14

Learning Without Limit-kinds of Learning **123**

Introduction 123
The Current Situation 125
Need for New Kinds of Learning 125
Different kinds of thinking and learning 126
Learning and the Brain 126
Critical Thinking 127
Thinking About One's Own Thinking and Learning 127
Effective Learning and Learning Styles 128
Conclusion 128

Bibliography of Learning: 129

15

Latest Technology For Teachers **131**

Introduction 131
The Flipped Class: What it is and what it is not 132
The Flipped Classroom is NOT 133
Transformational Potential of Flipped Classrooms 136
Advantages of Flipped Instruction 140
Final Thoughts on the Flipped Classroom 141
Flipping Increases Student Interaction 142
Flipping Changes the Way We Talk with Parents 143
References 144

16

Blended Learning **145**

Introduction 145
Building Innovations 147
Digital Literacy 147
Why learning through Digital mode in School Level? 149
Employability and Employable Generation 150
Current status of the Job Seekers 151
Blended Learning 151
Blended Learning – An inevitable Teaching Method 152
Acting Independently With the Digital Technology 153
Getting Accustomed in Handling Digital Tools 154
Creating Awareness of Technicalities of the Digital Tools 154
Using the Digital Tools for Communication and Learning Purpose 154
Acting Independently With the Digital Tools 155
Conclusion 155
References 156

17

Cloud Computing in Higher Education **157**

Introduction 157
Higher Education 158
Cloud Computing (CC) 159

Types of Cloud Computing 160
SaaS for education: Microsoft Live@edu 162
Cloud computing initiatives 162
IBM Cloud Academy 162
IEEE Cloud Computing 162
Amazon Web Services (AWS) 163
Google Apps 163
Microsoft Windows Azure 163
Education and the Cloud Computing 164
Advantages of Cloud Computing 165
Cloud Computing Based Education: Challenges and Issues 166
Conclusion 166
Reference 167

18

Effective Academic Excellence 169

Introduction 169
Conceptual Framework 171
Changing the learning process: 172
The key principles of Learning Environment of Tomorrow 174
Flexibility 174
The Learning Community 174
Classroom / Learning Studio 174
Group Learning Areas 174
Outdoor Learning Environment 175
Functional elements within a learning environment of tomorrow 176
Conclusion 176
References 177

19

Blended Learning 179

Introduction 179
Defining Blended Learning 181
The Growth of Blended Learning 183
The Appeal of Blended Learning 183
From a student perspective, the appeal of blended learning includes: 184
Format of Blended learning 184
Technology 184

Integration 185
Organization 185
Interaction 186
Student Expectations 186
Role of instructor in blended learning 186
Conclusion 187
References 188

20

Multimedia Programme in Perceiving Human Anatomy Among Students 189

Introduction 189
Review of Literature 192
Objectives 195
Methodology 195
Sample 195
Data Collection 195
Analysis and Interpretation 196
Performance of control group students between the pre test and post test in human anatomy 196
Suggestions 199
Conclusion 199
References 200

21

Role of ICT in Education 203

Introduction 203
Different Types of ICTs Their and in Education 203
Advantages of the Use of ICT in Education 205
Quick access to information 205
Easy availability of updated data: 205
Connecting Geographically dispersed regions: 206
Facilitation of learning 206
Catering to the Individual differences 206
Wider range of communication media 206
Facilitation of learning 207
Catering to the Individual differences: 207
Wider learning opportunities for pupils 207
Conclusion 207

References 208

22

Effective Blended Learning Practice **209**

Introduction 209
Teaching and Learning Strategies 210
Teacher Transitions and Professional Learning 210
Socialization 211
Tips For Succsess 211
Assessment 211
Feedback 211
Technology Instructions 211
Communication Policies or Protocols 212
Time Management 212
Academic Resources 213
Technical Resources 213
Conclusion 213
References 213

23

Blended Learning **215**

Introduction 215
History of Blended Learning 216
Advantages 216
Disadvantages 217
Models of Blended Learning 218
Flex Model 218
Enriched Virtual Model 219
Conclusions 221

24

Digi-class For Tomorrow **223**

Introduction 223
Why is digital technology essential in education? 224
Merits of Using Digital Technology 226
Demerits of Adapting Digital Technology in Present Day Education 227

Conclusion 228

25

Utility and Challenges of Blended Learning **229**

Introduction 229
Utilities of Blended learning 229
Better prepared students 230
Teaching 21st century skills 230
Less paperwork 230
All our teaching resources in one place 231
Lower costs 231
Better informed parents 231
Getting discussions going in class 231
Using Videos in Class and at Home 232
Social Media in a Safe Environment 232
Using Webcams for Revision 233
Different Learning Methods 233
Conclusion 234
References 235

26

Learning Environment of the Future Students **237**

Introduction 237
Open learning 238
E-learning 239
Open Learning through e-Learning 240
Conclusion 241
References 241

27

Attitude of Blended Learning Among Student–Teachers **243**

Research Studies 244
Need For the Study 244
Objectives of the Study 244
Hypotheses of the Study 245
Methodology Of The Study 245
Selection and Size of the Sample 245

Tool Development 245
Data Analysis 246
Findings of the Study 249
Conclusion 249
Reference 250

28

Teaching Aptitude and Teaching Practice Among Teacher Educators **251**

Introduction 251
Aptitude 252
Teaching Aptitude 252
Need for Blended Teaching 253
Blended Teaching Modes 254
Objectives 255
Hypothesis 255
Sample 256
Tools used for the study 256
Blended Teaching Possibilities 258
Implementation 259
Suggestions 260
Conclusion 261
References 262

29

Awareness Towards Utilizing Cell Phones For Students **263**

Introduction 263
Mobile Learning 263
Mobile Internet Browsers 264
M-learning in India 264
Mobile Communication Between Parents, Teachers and Students 264
Scope of the Study 265
Need of the Study 265
Review of Literature 265
Objectives of the Study 266
Hypothesis of the Study 266
Methodology 267
Samples For the Study 267
Tool Used For the Study 267

Scoring Procedure 267
Statistical techniques used 267
Analysis of the Data 267
Major Findings of the Study 269
Discussion 270
Educational Implication of the Study 270
Conclusion 271
References 271

30

Cloud Computing **273**

Introduction 273
Stone age to digital age 274
Types of cloud computing 274
How to operate? 275
Cloud computing in education world/Field 275
Conclusion 277
References 278

31

Effectiveness of E-content in Teaching **279**

Introduction 279
Need For the Study 280
E-content 281
Objectives of the Study 281
Methodology 281
Sampling Procedure 281
Hypotheses of the Study 281
Major Findings of the Study 283
Educational Implications of the Study 283
Conclusion 283
References 284

32

Blended Learning in Teacher Education **285**

Introduction 285
Definition of Blended Learning 286

Blended Learning 286
Road of Blended Learning 287
Blended Learning Equation 287
Why blend and what is being Blended? 287
Blended Learning a Boon for Personalizing Education 288
Merits in the implementation of Blended Learning 288
Demerits 289
Conclusion 289

33

Learning Environment of the Future Students **291**

Introduction 291
Open learning 292
E-learning 293
Open Learning through e-Learning 294
Conclusion 295
References 295

1

Revitalization of Science Teacher Education

Introduction

The present educational scenario of the 21st century has become prone to stress more on Quality than on Quantity. The primary aim of every educational institution is to provide a good and quality education to the students. Unless we built a strong base we cannot think over and strength of the premise. Similarly the country which shows keen interest in providing the quality based education will surely empower the knowledge of the students and in turn it will lead to the development of the Nation. Moreover this century is known for the drastic development of Science and Technology. Day by day numbers of innovations are keeping on growing. It is the duty of the teacher to incorporate recent developments to the students that occur across the world. With an increased availability of the knowledge centers and a rapid rise in the enrolment of the students the responsibilities of the teachers also have increased many folds. In case of science teacher, the responsibility becomes more than the others. Meanwhile if the teacher has enough capability to maintain the larger group of students, then he/she becomes the successful teacher. For this, it is mandatory for the Science teacher to equip, empower, and update the knowledge every day. In this connection the author of this paper has planned to discuss the present status of the Science teacher education and tries to give some suggestions that can improve the quality of the science education in India.

A few decades back the science was given a step-motherly treatment and was considered to be a subject meant for less important subject. Science has now established its claim to be placed in a school curriculum. Due to its utilitarian, intellectual, vocational, cultural moral and aesthetic values it has been placed in the curriculum with due prestige. The training, the student receives in science during his study days can be applied to solve other problems in future life. Moreover the results of the science are generalizable and it does not give any room for superstitions and other facts without proofs. Teacher education is the vital for the development of the country and this is the age of science and technology. Proper science education is must for the advancement of the nation. Several committees have forwarded their suggestions for the development of the teacher education in general and science education in particular, but the standard of science education in India is still to come up to international standard. Unfortunately the present day of teaching science is far from being satisfactory. The education of science teachers is the main concern to be geared up, organized, revitalized and improved in order to shape the science education in the light of the present changing scenario of the educational world.

Problems in Science Teacher Education

In the present science teacher education system the following problems have been identified.

1. Problems in selection of the candidates
2. Poor knowledge in preparing lesson plans
3. Lack of knowledge in preparing and handling teaching aids
4. Problems in supervision during practice teaching

Problems in Selection of the Candidates

In present condition, the selection of the candidates for B.Ed program are being done on the basis of their academic marks scored in the graduation level. It is not actually valid and reliable. In order to select the qualified candidates, the exclusive selection procedures have to be done through entrance examination. For example, the theory examination may be conducted for 50 marks and the other 50 marks can be allotted for the interview. The theory exam can comprise of general mental ability test, aptitude test, attitude test and general awareness. The interview can be of checking the personality of the candidate, interest of the candidate towards science subject and etc., this kind of selection will ensure the quality of science education and prevent the unwanted entry of the incapable or uninterested candidate into the program.

Poor Knowledge in Preparing Lesson Plans

Due to the short period of the B.Ed program, the student teachers gain inadequate knowledge in preparing the lesson plans. This will lead to the poor performance of the candidate during teaching practice. As a good science teacher, it is must to know the procedure of writing the lesson plan in effective manner. To overcome this problem, the special classes can be handled by the subject experts to provide adequate knowledge in preparing good lesson plans. Copying from the previous year's record books has to be avoided. The concerned faculty member has to look into this concern strictly to avoid such malpractices.

Lack of Knowledge in Preparing and Handling Teaching Aids

As we know that audio-visual aids promote the teaching learning process so that every science teacher must possess good capability in preparing and handling the teaching aids wherever necessary. Unfortunately, considerable number of student teachers are interested in buying the readymade teaching aids available in markets or prepared by the third person. This will lead to the financial burden as well as poor knowledge in preparing teaching aids. The subject teacher should not entertain this practices and he can ask the student teachers to prepare such teaching aids by their own. Teaching aids can be effectively prepared with the help of available low cost materials. Moreover the student teachers have to be trained to utilize the teaching aids in effective manner.

Problems in Supervision during Practice Teaching

Every student teacher undergoes for practice teaching for at least 45 days in B.Ed Program. During practice teaching, the subject teacher must supervise the candidate's way of motivating the students, way of delivering the concepts, way of giving necessary examples, way of using teaching aids and etc., Mistakes done by the student teacher can be corrected with the necessary instructions given by the subject teacher. But unfortunately, during practice teaching, the subject teachers could not find enough time to supervise each and every student teacher's teaching. In some institutions, during the practice teaching the subject teachers are assigned some official works or they take leave. This kind of thing should not be entertained. The authorities of institution should make strict measures in this concern.

Suggestions to Improve Science Teacher Education

1. The present one year B.Ed., program should be made of two years

2. Internship should be of six months instead of 45 days in practice teaching.
3. Scientific activities such as science fair, science club, museum, and exhibition can be encouraged.
4. College of education should be equipped with scientific materials and scientific instruments.
5. Seminars, conferences sand workshops related to science education can be organized every year by the institutions / colleges.
6. Job security should be provided to the selected and passed candidates by the government
7. Revision of curriculum should be made at a regular interval of time.
8. Suggestions from school science teacher and science teacher educators should be received in order to improve the system.
9. The teachers have to undergo for orientation programs, refresher courses every year in order to balance their ability with the recent developments.
10. The science teaching can be done with the help of innovative technologies like CAI, Video Packages etc., during the practice teaching.
11. Monitoring and evaluation should be made an integral part of teacher training program to know the strength, weakness, opportunities and Outcomes of the program.
12. All the existing college of educations should be accredited by NAAC.

Conclusion

In order to maintain the quality, the environment of the teacher education institutions should be improved. The science teacher educators should be given freedom to work. If there is any lacuna found in the system of such privately managed college of educations, their affiliations should be cancelled. NCTE is doing lot of commendable developments to improve the quality over nationwide. The relationship between the institution and the workers should be transparent and everyone should work to the betterment of the quality of education. In order to compete with the global knowledge market, the quality of education in our nation needs more betterment. This is becoming crucial for survival. So there is an urgent need to reform and revitalize the present education system for ensuring and creation of the quality of intellectual infrastructure in India.

References

1. Das, R.C. (1992): "Science teaching in Schools". Sterling Publishers private limited, New Delhi.
2. Deka, K.K. and Sharma, J.K. (1992): "Teacher education in the third world countries: India as a case study", The Educational Review, Chennai, pp. 201-205.
3. Krishna, D.G. and Rao, K.V.(1992) : "Effective Science Teaching: A trainers Paradigm", Journal of School science, NCERT, pp. 18-20.
4. Nadeen, N.A. (1989): Profile of Effective Teacher, Fulbright publishing company, Srinagar.
5. Panda B.N. & A.D.Tewari (2009): "Teacher Education", APH Publishing House, New Delhi. pp. 397-404.

2

Innovation in Teaching - Learning Process

Education is the most important invention of mankind. It is more important than his invention of tools, machines, spacecraft, medicine, weapons and even of language, because language too was the product of his education. Information Communication Technology is the most powerful engine to accelerate the growth of developing countries. It is evident to equip the young generation with the skills of ICT so that they will be fit to meet the challenges ahead of them. Today school children are well exposed to T.V. shows, computer programs, video games, e-mail based information exchange, internet browsing and many other forms of educative entertainment. Using the experiences of the children as the base, providing further learning experience is a challenging task

Computers are often a catalyst for student activity. Internet also known as cyberspace or information super highway plays a vital role in education. One of the most powerful and rewarding instructional material at the fingertips of the learner is the internet. Within seconds an entire civilization of the country thousands of miles away is at your desktop. Internet is also an ideal mechanism for encouraging students to assume responsibility for their own learning. As students find different learning resources on the internet, they become active participants in their quest for knowledge. Students are able to define their learning needs, find information, assess its value, build their own knowledge base, and communicate their discoveries.

Traditional classroom techniques will not do justice to the learners of this generation. They require technique that will stimulate them to explore, discover and learn by themselves as much as possible and the role of teacher is to be an effective facilitator. Teachers should have the freedom to innovate, to devise appropriate methods of communication and activities relevant to the needs and capabilities and the concerns of the community, says National Educational Policy. The quality of education we provide to our children depends in large measure upon the quality of teachers we inject into the educational system other things remaining equal. The quality of teachers in turn depends on the quality of preparation they receive in our teacher training institutions.

Modern media and education

We live in the age of computers. There are growing demands on almost everyone, including the learning and teaching community to become technologically literate. Computers are often a catalyst for student activity. Internet also known as cyberspace or information super highway plays a vital role in education. One of the most powerful and rewarding instructional material at the fingertips of the learner is the internet. Within seconds an entire civilization of the country thousands of miles away is at your desktop. Internet is also an ideal mechanism for encouraging students to assume responsibility for their own learning. As students find different learning resources on the internet, they become active participants in their quest for knowledge. Students are able to define their learning needs, find information, assess its value, build their own knowledge base, and communicate their discoveries.

The implementation of different branches of technology in the information and communication processing is called information communication technology. Their application in education includes web based learning, e-tutoring, computer assisted instruction, computer managed instruction, tele-conferencing, interactive video, multimedia learning, satellite instructional television programme, edusat, reach the unreached, virtual classroom, e-book, digital library and electronic community etc.

Web- based learning:

Web-based learning environments may be designed for students of distance education as well as conventional classroom students.

Principles of web-based learning

1. The learning experiences designed for web-based teaching must focus specific learning objectives and outcomes.
2. The learner should be actively engaged and made to feel the real-life experiences through simulation.
3. Keeping in mind the various learning styles of students, a variety of media are made use of to develop appropriately learning environment to achieve the desired learning out comes.
4. Learning environment must include both knowledge based as well as problem based learning.
5. Learning experiences must reflect the needs and interests of the community.

e-Learning

e-Learning includes different forms of technology enhanced learning such as online learning. E-learning is used to define a specific mode to attend a course or programmes of study where the students rarely or never meet face to face nor access on campus educational facilities, because they study online.

Advantages of e-learning

1. Improved performance – It has been proved that higher education students in online learning performed better than those in face to face courses.
2. Increased access – Instructors of the highest caliber can share their knowledge across borders, allowing students to attend courses across physical, political, and economic boundaries.
3. Convenience and flexibility to learners. In many contexts e-learning is self-paced and the learning sessions are available 24x7. Learners are not bound to a specific day or time to physically attend classes. They can also pause learning sessions at their convenience.

e-tutoring

e-tutoring can be defined as teaching, support, management and assessment of students on programmes of study that involves significant use of online technology. Thus at first glance e-tutoring is only different to tutoring in terms of the involvement of technology. Herein, however, are contained vital differences in terms of time, distance and the specific technologies adopted, and these are all the Implications for teaching staff. The capabilities required can be quiet different to face to face teaching both in terms of integrating appropriate forms of technology into learning activities and in managing and supporting students' learning online .

Computer Assisted instruction (CAI)

In Computer Assisted Instruction, the lesson and its continents to be learnt are recorded in the software of the computer. The software in the form a C.D. or cassette is inserted in the computer and when the student presses the keys in the keyboard, lessons appear in the monitor as small texts, each followed by a question. The student has to answer the questions by pressing the keys and the answers to appear in the monitor screen. If answer given by the student matches with the answer provided in the study material booted, it will be acknowledged and he is allowed to proceed further. If the given answer is incorrect, he is given alternate explanations or asked to study the same frame again before answering the question. In this way the computer manages the response of the individual learner.

Merits of Computer Assisted Instruction

1. The learner can receive the content very fast and that too without any error.
2. As the quality of learning material presented is rich, with animation and appropriate background sound, interest for learning is kindled.
3. Since the learner himself operates his computer and learns, learning interest is sustained throughout the session.
4. The computer successfully manages the different responses of the learner by directing him appropriately what to do further.
5. The content of the lesson cold be presented as text, diagrams or in animated forms.

6. Based on the learner's achievement, the computer will decide the nature of his further learning.
7. Computer can act according to the speed of the learner and his learning needs.
8. The computer can help any number of students to learn humpty number of times, without getting tired unlike a teacher. The same learning package can be repeatedly used for any number of times.
9. The quality of the study materials could be upgraded in a short span of time.
10. The cost and labour involved in providing computer assisted instruction though appears to be high in the beginning, it works out to be cheaper when we take into account its repeated use and the present cost of educating a student through teacher –centered methods.

Computer Managed Learning (CML)

Unlike CAI, wherein computer is used in tutorial work CML makes use of the computer in a different role in instruction. In CML the main role of the computer is record keeping and it does not provide any direct instruction to the leaner. It takes over the other responsibilities of the teacher like evaluating the response sheets of students, gathering and sharing information about each learner and updating the same periodically, finding the resource options available for every individual student to learn a topic, monitoring the learning of the student while he is making use of the instructional programme selected to suit his potentials and directing the learners what to do next. This type of instruction, though indirect, helps to assess the learner's present level of knowledge, weakness or gaps in his learning and remedial action possible.

Tele-Conferencing

In Tele-Conferencing, people situated at distant places establish direct contact through tele-communication and converse among themselves. In a tele-conferencing procedure all the three types of tele-conferencing such as audio, video and computer is integrated and supplements each other so that the participants get almost the feeling as if they are present physically in the conference.

Virtual- Education

Virtual education is a term describing online education using the internet. It refers to instruction in a learning environment where teacher and student are separated by time or space, or both, and the teacher provides course content through course management applications, multimedia resources, the internet, videoconferencing, etc. Students receive the content and communicate with the teacher via the same technologies.

Virtual course is similar to online course which is delivered on the internet. "Virtual" is used here to characterize the fact that the course is not taught in a classroom face to face but through some substitute mode that can be associated with classroom teaching that means people do not have to go to the real class to learn. A virtual programme is a study program in which all courses or at least a significant portion of the courses are virtual courses.

A virtual classroom is a learning environment created in the virtual space. The virtual classrooms improve access to advanced educational experiences by allowing students and instructors to participate in remote learning communities using personal computers; and to improve the quality and effectiveness of education by using the computer to support a collaborative learning process. The explosion of the knowledge age has changed the context of what is learnt and how it is learnt – the concept of virtual classrooms is a manifestation of this knowledge revolution.

Instruction Modes for Virtual Education

1. Video-based courses are like face-to-face classroom courses, with a lecturer speaking and PowerPoint slides or online examples used for illustration. Video-streaming technologies are used. Students watch the video by means of freeware or plug-ins (e.g. windows media player, real player).

2. Audio-based courses are similar but instead of moving pictures only the sound track of the lecturer is provided. Often the course pages are enhanced with a text transcription of the lecture.

3. Animated courses: enriching text-oriented or audio-based course material by animations is generally a good way of making the content and its appearance more interesting.

4. Web-supported textbook courses are based on specific textbooks. Students read and reflect on the chapters by themselves. Review questions, topics for discussion, exercises, case studies, etc. are given chapter wise on a website and discussed with the lecturer.

5. Peer-to-peer courses are courses taught "on-demand" and without a prepared curriculum. A new field of online education has emerged in 2007 through new online education platforms.

Homework assignments are normally submitted electronically, e.g. as an attachment on e-mail or uploaded to the system in a view complete. When help is needed, lecturers, tutors, or fellow students, or a help desk are available, just like in a real university, the difference is that all communication goes via electronic media.

Advantages of virtual education

Cyber School economizes time and cost, as the student does not require traveling to a real classroom to learn. Online learning creates the opportunity for integrating digital media into the curriculum in an interactive format making teaching and learning more students –centered regular full time students, distance education students, and in fact any one learning through cyber schools need not go in search of libraries to gather needed information. Online learning promotes self-learning, critical thinking and problem solving skills.

Conclusion

In modern days media play a vital role in education. Virtual schools now exist all around the world. Some of these virtual schools have been integrated into public schools, where students sit in computer laboratory and do their work online. In other situations students can be completely home schooled, or they can take any combination of public or private home schooling and online classes.

Enlightened, emancipated and empowered teachers lead communities and nations in their march towards better and higher quality of life. They reveal and elaborate the secrets of attaining higher values in life and nurture empathy for the fellow beings. Teachers are the torch bearers in creating social cohesion, national integration and a learning society. They not only disseminate knowledge but also create and generate new knowledge. They are responsible for acculturating role of education. No nation can even marginally slacken its efforts in giving necessary professional inputs to its teachers and along with that due status to their stature and profession.

References

1. Andrews, R. (ed.) (2004), the Impact of ICT on Literacy Education. London, RoutledgeFalmer.
2. Cox, M. (1997), The Effects of Information Technology on Students' Motivation. Coventry, Council for Educational Technology.

3

Flipped Classrooms Learning

Introduction

The "flipped classroom" has been making waves in the educational world for some time now. The concept of the flipped classroom has become one of the hottest debates in the academic world among primary educators, professors, and administrators alike. As education-based technology and online platforms continue to grow and improve, more and more devices, programs, and concepts are entering the educational world and shaking things up. Where at one time the concept of online learning, computer-based assignments, and the virtual classroom were scoffed at, today online education and technology in the classroom are top priorities for schools, teachers, and researchers.

Within our increasingly digital world, most of us agree that education must respond to the changing atmosphere of society. We accept that online learning and certain academic technologies are worthwhile. However, with education and learning, this flipped classroom remains both positives and negatives to the approach.

One of the hottest trends in education today is the flipped classroom: Computer-savvy students turn to online videos for the content normally taught in class and use class time to collaborate in discussion with peers and instructors. A flipped classroom is fundamentally about upending of time on task. Instead of holding forth each day at the front of a classroom the traditional notion of the "sage on a stage" teachers convert their lectures to videos, slide shows or audio lessons that can be watched or heard by students at home or elsewhere via the Internet or other information transfer tools, such as DVDs and thumb drives.

Flipped classroom education

The reason flipped classrooms are improving education around the world is because the role of the teacher has been flipped from a lecturer to a tutor. The focus of the classroom transforms one-size fits all instruction into individualized coaching.

What Does a Flipped Classroom Look Like?

Flipped Classroom will certainly look very different from a traditional classroom. Instead of students sitting in individual desks facing the front while their teacher lectures, students sit at tables or desks pushed together or are off by themselves doing work. Students are out of their seats, accessing books, computers and others students for information. Although a Flipped Classroom may appear chaotic, loud, or even messy at first glance, the action and collaboration taking place in this non-traditional classroom is a direct result of student learning. Have fun physically setting up your classroom for a flip by providing areas for group and individual learning and don't forget to involve students in the new Flipped Classroom design.

Flipped Classroom Model

The flipped classroom model is revolutionizing teaching

methods and strategies around the globe, addressing these concerns by creating time for individualized 1:1 instruction between teachers and students. Flipped classrooms are a reversed teaching model that "flips" the settings for instruction and homework. In a flipped class, instruction is provided to students at home through video or Internet based lectures and class time is used to complete homework-like assignments. By moving instruction to the home and homework to the class, students are given more 1:1 time with their teacher to work through their assignments. This 1:1 time helps to ensure that each student fully understands the key concepts presented in each lesson plan before moving on to the next lesson.

Here's how it works

1. Teachers provide students with digital instruction to watch at home (or after school)
2. Students watch the instruction to familiarize themselves with concepts to be covered in class the following day
3. Students spend class time completing assignments, based on the previous night's instruction, with the assistance of teachers
4. Students with a firm grasp of the lesson are encouraged to move on, and students who need assistance have a teacher readily available to help

Benefits of flipped classroom

1. More efficient for teachers: While there is an initial up-front investment that teachers have to make to set up a flipped classroom – creating a video can take 15 minutes or two days – they can ultimately save a lot of time using this model. In the future, recorded lesson plans and collected resources can be easily transferred to other classes. Plus, if students miss a class, teachers don't have to spend time going over missed material because it's all online.

2. Students control their learning: Research has shown that we all learn in different ways and at different speeds. If students are learning content at home, they can take their time to read through a passage, re-watch a video lecture or even initiate a Google search to better understand an idea. Instructors can also post multiple kinds of materials so that students are more likely to find a source that will help them, whether it's an article, video or interactive tool.

3. Inexpensive for schools to implement: Besides investing in a new video cameras or better classroom computers, the only other thing you need is time. This model is much more cost-effective for schools than purchasing hundreds of new classroom gadgets to increase engagement.

4. Versatile, engaging way to share content: One of the greatest things about this model is that teachers can share so many different kinds of content. Learning isn't restricted to a whiteboard or textbook. Instead, students can be directed to any website, mobile application or other kind of content. Teachers can create learning modules that allow students to quickly jump from one resource to the next.

5. Students—including special education students—having difficulty with concepts can pause and rewind the videos to give themselves extra time to parse out what a teacher means. "That's one of the most powerful things about these videos: that students who process slower, can process slower,"

Administrator role in implementing flipped learning

"Absolutely, they are critical as instructional leaders and lead learners in their schools,"

"They can support innovation, provide collaborative time and professional development, assign resources to innovative teachers, communicate with parents about new teaching strategies, and provide feedback and a view from outside the classroom.

The primary reason administrators balk at flipped learning is a lack of familiarity: "They need more information about how it works the issues that come up like how to evaluate flipped-learning teachers, the problems of rolling it out." Administrators says that flipped learning can greatly increase a teacher's ability to provide differentiated instruction given that students work at their own pace in the classroom—and teachers can provide more challenging work for those who are breezing through.

Administrators also continue to support the use of video within instruction and believe that it has an important role within classrooms today and tomorrow. Approximately one quarter of school principals indicated that their teachers are using videos they found online or creating their own Videos as part of their flipped learning model implementation. And thinking ahead to the next generation of classroom teachers, some of the principals said that they want pre service teachers to learn how to create and use videos and other digital media within their teacher preparation programs.

Advantage of flipped classroom learning

1. Students are able to approach material and take it in at their own speed. By covering lecture material at home and from a video-based platform, students can privately view the material. This allows them to approach things at their own pace without worry of peers noticing them moving slower or faster. Students can stop, pause, rewind, and fast forward material so that they can examine things in their own way.

2. By taking the lecture portion of the classroom home with them, students are able to utilize their teachers' one-on-one attention more successfully in the classroom. Students sit through lecture, gather questions, and prepare themselves for the day with the teacher to tackle "homework". Because the actual exercises are done in the classroom rather than at home with this model, students have their teacher available for questions with problems when they occur.

3. The flipped classroom also allows teaching to adapt more easily to the different teaching styles that individual students may be most successful with. By putting lectures in a video format, students can listen to the lesson and watch the video illustrate the lesson. Of course, this largely depends on how successful the actual video lecture is. You want a lecture (like the Khan videos) that explains concepts verbally, but also draws them out in images and pictures. This provides adequate learning opportunities for verbal learners and for visual learners. With in-classroom lecturing, the visual aspect of lecturing can be significantly more difficult to accomplish.

Disadvantage of flipped classroom learning

1. Classroom lecturing works better for some and doesn't work for others; the flipped classroom method is not going to accommodate every individual perfectly. The biggest setback today to the flipped classroom method is that not all students and schools have access to technologies that can really work for this method.

2. Students from lower income areas and lower income families may not have access to the computers and internet technologies that the flipped classroom requires. The structure really hinges on every student having personal access to his or her own personal device. This simply is not the case for every student and every school district. Students who do not have personal home

computers or access to the internet would be forced to use public computers at a library or at the school. This, to some degree, eliminates the personal and private experience of taking in the lecture. What makes having lectures as homework so powerful is that students can do it on their own time and in their own way. At a library computer or school computer time limits typically exist and access can be limited if it is busy. This is problematic.

3. Another downside to the idea of the flipped classroom that many people bring up is the fact that students would be spending all of their "homework time" plugged-in in front of a computer screen. Not only do not all students do well with learning from a screen, but this also adds to a student's time in front of a screen and sitting inactively. While this concern isn't singular to the flipped classroom, the teaching concept doesn't help our young students to get up and get away from their computers, televisions, and iPods.

Conclusion

Flipped classroom learning are shifting the way teachers provide Instruction by inverting traditional teaching methods to engage students in the learning process. Using technology, lectures are moved out of the classroom and delivered online as a means to free up class time for interaction and collaboration. In order to effectively implement a flipped classroom, teachers must possess a set of requisite technical skills, conceptual knowledge and pedagogical expertise.

References

1. Bergmann, J., J. Overmyer, and B. Wilie. 2011. "The Flipped Class: Myths Vs. Reality." http://www.thedailyriff.com/articles/the-flipped-class-conversation-689.php.
2. Hertz, M. 2012. "The Flipped Classroom: Pro and Con."

Edutopia. http://www.edutopia.org/blog/flipped-classroom-pro-and-con-mary-beth-hertz.

3. Makice, K. 2012. "Flipping the Classroom Requires More Than Video | GeekDad | Wired.com." *GeekDad.* http://www.wired.com/geekdad/2012/04/flipping-the-classroom/.

4. Strayer. 2007. "The Effects of the Classroom Flip on the Learning Environment: a Comparison of Learning Activity in a Traditional Classroom and a Flip Classroom That Used an Intelligent Tutoring System". Thesis, Ohio State University. http://etd.ohiolink.edu/view.cgi/Strayer%20Jeremy.pdf?osu1189523914.

5. Strayer, J. 2011. "The Flipped Classroom: Turning the Traditional Classroom on Its Head." http://www.knewton.com/flipped-classroom/.

4

Role of ICT in Educational Transactions

Introduction

The role of teachers is enormous, especially for nurturing children in their formative years, when they begin their schooling. Hence, it is very crucial to have qualified teachers to ensure prefect development of students. The various objectives of the ICT in Teacher Education, are to provide high quality education, monitor Teacher Education as approved by National Council for Teacher Education at all levels in the State, to develop research facilities in Teacher Education; The Tamil Nadu Teacher Education University from 2008, is very much focused to promote quality in Education and to standardize the system of operation. This paper focused on EDUSAT, INSAT, SITE, CAI, Video Conferencing, Virtual Classroom and the equipments and the UGC Tele programmes. Whatever it me, the today's student teachers are tomorrow's Teachers. So that, we are in need of utilization of media and technology in out classrooms and it can used in future for our educational transactions.

Teachers play a vital role in the overall growth and development of students. Teaching as profession is not only restricted to imparting academic knowledge, but also inculcating the right principles and values to the students. The role of teachers is enormous, especially for nurturing children in their formative years, when they begin their schooling. Hence, it is very crucial to have qualified teachers to ensure prefect development of students. Today, there are enormous colleges and universities in India that offer Courses in Education and Teacher Science.

As the needs of primary students are completely different from secondary students, the primary teachers and the secondary teachers are required to take different teachers 'training courses. Hence, most of the prominent Teacher training institutes offer different Courses which include Junior Basic Training or JBT, Basic Training Certificate or BTC, Primary Teachers Training or PTT, Bachelor of Education or B.Ed, Diploma in Education or D.Ed, and many other teachers training courses.

National Council of Teacher Education was established in 1973 by the Govt. of India. It was formed as advisory organization to government, on issues related to the teacher education. The government formed a National Policy on Education in 1986, which was aimed at setting up statutory body to provide quality Teachers' training in country, as step towards producing quality teaching professionals in India. In the year 1995, NCTE was awarded the status of statutory body in the pursuance of the National Council for Teacher Education Act. This Council sets the standards and norms for teachers' training right from primary teacher's education to post graduation teachers education. In the past, a teacher who wanted to display information for a classroom full of students had only a few options at his disposal: writing everything out on the chalkboard manually or projecting it onto a screen using a transparency projector. Today, the liquid crystal display (LCD) technology becoming common in homes has also made its way into the classroom.

Utilization of EDUSAT in Schools of Tamil Nadu

The NCERT acts as a major agency for implementing the bilateral Cultural Exchange Programmes with other countries in the field of school education also in addition to research, development, training, extension, and publication and dissemination activities. INSAT (Indian National Satellites) are a series of satellites projected and maintained by ISRO for multipurpose space applications. INSAT-3B, INSAT-3C are satellites in this series.

The ISRO launched a Satellite for education, termed as EDUSAT. With the launch of EDUSAT, TV, Radio and data transfer has become easy for educational institutions situated all over the country. Quality education is to be provided to school students especially in rural areas through this Satellite. This will also enable high quality in-service training to school teachers in the state. Live programmes are being broadcast through the studio at Anna University using EDUSAT. For proper utilization of EDUSAT, a plan of action has been formulated. Satellite Interactive Terminals have been set up in all 29 District Institutes of Education and Training. Satellite interactive terminals will be established in all the BRCs, 215 Urban Cluster Resource Centres and 2000 Government High and Higher Secondary Schools in this academic year 2006-2007 in a phased manner under the aegis of SSA.

Some schools like Delhi Public School and IGNOU are already experimenting with teaching through lessons prepared for distance teaching using multimedia, slides etc. The communication technology based teaching is a viable solution. Any institution which can afford and is willing to put the efforts and costs involved, can utilize the technology. But the technology is still quite expensive and state has to support the venture. Of course the country may look forward to the institutions that have expertise in the related fields at the right time, for the better utilization.

SITE and its Uses

Satellite Instructional Television Experiment (SITE) (1975).This project, one of the largest techno-social experiments in human communication, was commissioned for the villagers and their Primary School going children of selected 2330 villages in six states of India. It started on August 1, 1975 for a period of one year in six states Rajasthan, Karnataka, Orissa, Bihar, Andhra Pradesh and Madhya Pradesh. The main objectives of this experiment were to study the process of existing rural communications, the role of television as new medium of education, and the process of change brought about by the community television in the rural structure with following two type of telecast: (i) Developmental education programmes in the area of agriculture and allied subjects, health, family planning and social education, which were telecast in the evening for community viewing and (ii) The school programmes of 22 ½ minutes duration each in Hindi, Kannada, Oriya and Telugu were telecast on each school day for rural primary school children of 5- 12 years age group to make the children realize the importance of science in their day to day life.

SITE experiment showed that the new technology made it possible to reach number of people in the remotest areas. The role of television was appreciated and it was accepted in rural primary schools as an educational force (IGNOU, 2000). Post-SITE project (1977).The target group for this post SITE project was the villagers of Rajasthan. This was a SITE continuity project and was initiated in March 1977 when a terrestrial transmitter was commissioned at Jaipur. The main objectives of SITE continuity project were to; (i) Familiarize the rural masses with the improved and scientific know how about farming, the use of fertilizers and the maintenance of health and hygiene; (ii) Bring about national and emotional integration; and (iii) Make rural children aware of the importance of education and healthy environment. This project was also successful.

Mass media serve some important functions. They are helpful in teaching large number of people. They are helpful in the spread of compulsory education and adult literacy. Recently their use is being made increasingly in distance education. They are useful in making instructions more effective and meaningful. Mass media play a pivotal role in education. It may be hardware approach like radio, tape recorder, television etc or soft ware approach like newspapers books , magazines etc. Mass media include Computer, Educational satellite, VCR and T.V to meet the tremendous challenges in the educational field using of multimedia is inevitable. In fact it is essential for the ever changing educational field.

The Barriers to Verbal Classroom Communication in the Classroom are;

1. Inaudibility of speech
2. Abnormal speed of speech
3. Unfamiliar pronunciation of the teacher.
4. Use of unfamiliar words and technical terms without explanations
5. Lack of understanding of the basic knowledge of the students known as referent confusion
6. Day dreams on the part of the students on account of their inattentiveness.
7. Unsystematic presentation of the subject matter
8. Lack of scope of immediate feedback
9. Lack of physical facilities in the classroom
10. Socio-economic and cultural difference among the students.

CAI

One of the significant instructional applications of computers is "Computer Assisted Instruction" (CAI). It is nothing but giving instruction with the help of computers. In CAI, the activity of the learner is the most important attribute. The computer can be helping the teacher in the following areas;

i) Evaluation of students performance and classification of children according to abilities;

ii) Preparation of time-table and class schedule;

iii) Allocation of learning materials according to individual needs and interests.

iv) Maintenance of progress cards efficiently and confidentially.

v) Providing information and large data for guidance and reference.

vi) Provision of direct interaction between pupils and subject matter.

vii) Engaging students in tutorial work;

viii) Providing immediate feedback to students for better interaction and motivation

ix) Developing the CAI programmes to teach their students individually.

x) Using the Internet related activities and to take print outs and documentation to their students.

Video Conferencing

Videoconferencing can provide two way interactive teaching-learning facilities where the students can interact with highly qualified faculties from distant locations. This also reduces the costs involved in travel and energy. The visual contents should be used to furnish illustrations during the conferencing of the lecture, to permit pupils to experience the content through the avenues of sight and learning.

Virtual Classroom

Virtualizing is the creation of a three-dimensional, interactive model of a problem or dataset to find a virtual solution that will also work in the real world. Virtual reality also has the flexibility to be a tremendous aid for design in the areas of engineering and manufacturing, architecture and construction, biotechnology and nano pharmacology, chemistry and modeling molecules, medicine and bionics, the apparel sector, and the fine arts. Three-dimensional models of molecules and living structures may be fabricated and handled virtually. Electronics may be fabricated and tested absent creation of a physical prototype. Virtual modeling clay can be shaped into various forms for either aesthetic or practical purposes Computer-artificially constructed objects and worlds should conform with reasonable accuracy to the tangible and other laws that shape such things and environments in the actual world. Some divergence might be relevant for surreal applications, but in case the difference is too great then the sense of believability is lost. Some of the Virtual Classroom Equipments are;

1. E-D Wireless 3D Glasses for the PC
2. VirtualFX 3D TV Converter
3. 3DPlus 2D to 3D DVD Software
4. 3D Combine 2D to 3D Photo Software
5. 3D DVDs for your PC or TV
6. Long Range Viewing Equipment for Stereo Projection

7. InFocus DepthQ 3D Video Projector
8. 3D Glasses for Samsung and Mitsubishi Televisions
9. Vuzix - VR920 Head Mounted Display

SITE

The satellite instructional television experiment was launched in our country in august 1975. The main Objective of the SITE programmes was to help people in their development endeavours. The major educational objective of INSAT television is to promote alternative approaches to education for children, youth and adults.

INSAT

INSAT (Indian National Satellites) are a series of satellites projected and maintained by ISRO for multipurpose space applications. INSAT-3B, INSAT-3C are satellites in this series. The objective of the INSAT (Indian National Satellite - 1982) project was aimed at making the rural masses aware of the latest developments in the areas of agricultural productivity, health and hygiene.

EDUSAT

At present, using EDUSAT, networks for many user agencies like IGNOU, CEC/UGC, CIET/NCERT, AICTE, Blind People's Association (BPA) or Blind school, Karnataka school network, VTU, YCMOU, Goa University, Amrita VRC, and Kerala/Tamil Nadu are operational for a total of about 1200 terminals or classrooms.

UGC Country wide Classroom

The University Grants Commission (UGC) was formally established only in November 1956 as a statutory body of the Government of India through an Act of Parliament for the coordination, determination and maintenance of standards of university education in India.

CLASS Project

A Pilot Project on Computer Literacy and Studies in Schools (CLASS) was initiated in 1984-85 in 248 selected Secondary/ Higher secondary schools. The objective is to acquaint students and teachers with the wide range of computer applications and its potential as a learning medium. By the end of 1988-89 about 2600 schools had been covered. Sixty resource centers had been set up to train school teachers and provide support to the participating schools. Efforts have been made to start generation of indigenous software through NCERT, New Delhi. The project is jointly co-coordinated and supported by the Department of Electronics, the Department of Education, Computer Maintenance Corporation (CMC) and the NCERT.

Learning without Frontiers" (LWF)

It represents UNESCO's pro-active response to addressing the deep social and political problems that confront humanity as they relate to the role of learning in society. It views the processes of engaging in collaborative, multi channel and innovative learning as being critical for both the development of the individual and the building and linking of culturally diverse communities.

Conclusion

Reliable wireless service is has become an essential tool in both enhancing the education of electronic based teaching learning students as well as increasing operational productivity at SMART schools. Recent advances in Wi-Fi technology dramatically increase the range and reliability of Wi-Fi services by automatically focusing and directing signals over the fastest RF paths as the environment changes. A lot of modern classrooms are replacing classic white boards with “Smart boards”. These smart boards are usually touch screen and are connected to a computer. This means that anything on the computer can be shown to an entire class relatively easily. Smart boards do require projectors and can be quite expensive; also environmental effects such as glare through windows can affect use. Everyone should show responsibility towards the LCD projector utility in their classrooms. To fulfill this objective we should educate our all teachers through this electronic technology. The management and authorities should initiates to use videos, documentary films and technology related magazines etc to build LCD projectors knowledge among teachers and develop the educational transactions.

References

1. Edwards, Julie-Ann, M. Hartnell and R. Martin (2002) Interactive Whiteboards: Some Lessons for the Classroom, Micro math, summer 2002, pp 30-33.

2. Gueissaz, Albert. (2002), New Tool, New Actors, New Decisions, European Journal of Education, Vol.37, No.1, p. 16-21.

3. Jo Towers (2007) Using video in teacher education, Canadian Journal of Learning and Technology. Volume 33, No.2 Spring 2007. pp. 54-58.

4. Mark Fischetti (November 2007) Two Technologies Shine, Scientific American, Inc: pp. 110–111

5. Nachimuthu, K. (2007), Mobile learning and Distance Education, Journal of Distance Education, University of Jammu, Kashmir, India, 2007, Vol. XII, No:1, pp. 33-39.

6. Solvie, Pamela A (2004) Digital Whiteboard: A Tool in Early

Literacy Instruction. Reading Teacher, Vol. 57, No.5, pp.: 484–487.

7. Vijayakumari, G. et al., (2008), Quality issues and standards of E-content, Journal of Educational Technology, I-Manager Pub, Vol. 04, No. 03, Oct- Dec 2007, pp. 8-11.

8. Wu, C. H. and Lin, T. Y. (2000) Education terms: knowledge economy, knowledge management, Education information and research Journal, Vol.37, pp.100-101.

5

Quality Enhancement in Teaching – Learning

Introduction

Using the technology developments is an important thing for teaching learning process. Now a day's the internet and other Medias are doing a vital role for teaching learning process. Using these technologies is easy to understand the concepts of teaching for the students. Digital projectors are the most exciting classroom tool ever. A picture truly is worth a thousand words. Project your laptop or desktop image on the screen for students to see you solve that math problem.

A good teacher is continually learning. Technology makes it easy to extend your learning by offering professional development on demand. Professional development will keep your teaching fresh, current, and will remind you of what it is like to learn something new. Teachers who are continually teach make empathetic teachers they understand how frustrating it can be to learn something for the first time.

Develop a Personal Learning Network on Twitter

Twitter is an excellent place for new teachers to connect, collaborate, share ideas, and struggles with educators around the world. When joining Twitter, make sure to fill out your profile with information related to education. This will help others in education find you. http://twitter4teachers.pbworks.com to find other educators that teach in the same content area(s). Be sure to add your Twitter name to the appropriate list so that other educators can find you.

Keep Students Engaged

Always have engaging activities on hand to keep your students on task and learning. Students will misbehave if they have nothing to do, don't give them the opportunity to be bored. Technology is a great way to fill those extra minutes with critical thinking and problem solving activities. Keep a list or bookmark folder full of great online logic puzzle and problem solving websites for students to refer to when they have extra minutes.

Keep Yourself Organized

During the first year of teaching you will find a lot of new great resources, keep track of all these great finds in one easy to manage location. Delicious.com is a bookmarking website that allows you to bookmark and organize websites and web tools as you find them. Bookmarks can be collected and shared with others educators through Delicious. Be sure to install the Internet browser plug in so that you can easily bookmark a site with the click of a button.

Communicate with e-mail and Blogs

Email facilitates communication with all three members of the academic triangle: the teacher, the student and the parent.

The beauty of email is that you can dash off a really short note which will be read. Blogs are a wonderful way to keep an electronic journal which encourages comment and dialog with your students. Anything which helps a student express his thoughts has to be a good thing. Post your assignments on a Web portal. Parents will thank you for this information. They love to be able to review their children's assignments and grades online. The more you can involve parents, the more successful your outcomes will be.

Incorporate a Digital Projector into your Lessons

Digital projectors are the most exciting classroom tool ever. A picture truly is worth a thousand words. Project your laptop or desktop image on the screen for students to see you solve that math problem.

Conclusion

Remember: you are a teacher! You are in the business of igniting the fires of curiosity. Take your own medicine as you probe, inquire and learn about these exciting technologies. The Internet had its birth in the research and academic communities. It was created to allow the free and rapid flow of information to benefit higher learning. Let's recapture that focus in our work, and enrich our teaching in the process.

References

1. Annaraja, P. (2000) "Information technology and Education" in Reflections on Education, St. Xavier's college of Education, Palaymakotai.
2. Aggarwal,J.C (2008), Principles of Methods and Techniques of Teaching. APH Publishers, New Delhi.
3. Kirshnamacharyulu, V (2004), To be sure teaching for Teacher's Today & Tomorrow.

6

Use of ICT For Teaching Psychology

Introduction

ICT enriches the campus by incorporating its role well. This is present paper illustrates the use of ICT in various ways in teaching Psychology for students of B.Ed., Course. An attempt is made to analyze how technology could be best incorporated to the maximum benefit for the students. The purpose of this paper is to create awareness about the advantages of using ICT in a classroom and to illustrate how and when to use them effectively. This information can also be used in developing e-content or module for core paper II of Tamilnadu Teachers Education University B.Ed., syllabus namely Psychology of Learning and Human development.

In the present educational scenario, ICT (Information and Communication Technology) is considered as an important tool in the entire educational system – curriculum, instruction and management. Class room instruction forms the basis for majority of educational processes. Hence it should aim at making the teaching learning process interesting, effective and goal oriented. In current scenario of a classroom there is a paradigm shift in the focus from teacher centered approach to child centered approach, autocratic classroom climate to democratic climate, lecture method to constructive activity, stress full learning to joyful learning, general learning to customized learning, teacher or instructor to facilitator. The advantages of using ICT are dealt with under the broad four categories, namely 1. As an aid-to augment the learning process 2. As an administrative tool-to effectively undertake other curricular transactions like administrating tests, evaluation, maintenance of records and many more. 3. As a subject per see to learn about ICT, thought it is only incidental in psychology class 4. As a medium of knowledge management – use a range of strategies and practices to create, identify, represent and distribute insights and experiences. The present study elaborate some ways and means to convert a traditional B.Ed., Psychology class room in to a smart class and mentions the advantages associated with it.

ICT as a Learning Process

In the B.Ed., Psychology syllabus prescribed by Tamilnadu Teachers Education University there are ten units. The uses of multimedia are discussed here unit wise. In the first unit concepts about the various methods and branches of psychology can be easily illustrated by preparing power points by downloading pictures and images from the internet. Pictures, images or schemes are available in plenty for topics on S-R conditioning, Thorndike's puzzle box and Pavlov's classical conditioning. If the teacher is persistent enough she could get picture with beautiful animation too. The only problem the teacher face is the problem of plenty which could be easily overcome by the teacher developing a scanning eye with practice. Using visual perception it become easier for the students to distinguish conditioned stimulus from unconditioned stimulus, conditioned responds from unconditioned responds. Various website offer a large number of methods of psychology. For example a more look at the simple figure, the student is able to graphs the importance of the whole against the parts. The ice berg model of personality structure of Sigmund Freud's Psychoanalysis theory is well illustrated in many website. All that the teacher requires to do is to cut and paste these figures and make a presentation with notes of explanations. There are websites which offer Transactional Analysis well illustrated by schematic representations which rarely finds a place in many of the popular text books followed in B.Ed., colleges.

Another strategy to improve the understanding ability of the students is that different unit of Educational Psychology can be compared easily using a table with the Colum heading as' unit wise objective, concept, variation, main ideas and method adopted'. The topic of the units of Psychology namely "Nature of Educational Psychology, Human Growth and Development, Cognitive Development, Social, Emotional and Moral Development, Learning, Intelligence and Creativity, Motivation and Group Dynamics, Personality and Assessment, Mental Health and Hygiene and Guidance and Counseling from the row headings this table will provide the summary of all unit the Educational Psychology. To add value to this table, pictures of the ten units can be pasted. It would serve as the ready beckoner for the exam oriented students.

Once the various approaches in psychology are made clear to the students by making use of ICT enabled instructional materials the major difficulties in getting through the other concepts in the minds of the students become easier for the teacher on one hand .On the other hand the students can easily go through this comprehensive table understand, appreciate, recall and recite. Since these are objectives most often tested in our present system of examination this in our present system of examination this would serve them the purpose. Similarly, the concept of Identical twins. Fraternal Twins, Mendelism, Sex determination in human being, the difference between positive reinforcement, negative reinforcement and punishment all these can be made easy by an ingenious teacher. One may argue that good books are available with excellent illustrations and figures. But most of the time a single book will not be giving the best illustration for all the concepts. But teacher can collect the best illustration, best images and best tables from the various freely downloadable sites and make her own presentation in a LCD projector. Over and above, already prepared PowerPoint's are also available for many of the topics which the classroom teacher can alter according to the needs of the students. In this context the uses of the free open source community based tool 'Moodle' cannot be overemphasized. This tool can be used effectively to speed up the process of learning among the students.

ICT- as an Administrative Tool

The uses of computer especially the packages MS office is tremendous in a classroom as an administrative tool. It is a boon to the classroom teacher. It is used for marking the attendance register, calculating the attendance percentage for issue of hall tickets, giving roll numbers or register numbers, preparation of question papers, preparation of key, entry of marks, maintaining rank card or progress report or a cumulative record.

ICT as a Subject

Even though it is in the purview of Engineering and technology students, the basic operations of the computer, knowledge about various tools, utilities and sites available are a must for any teacher. By using modern gadgets as tool in a classroom the students are bound to learn about them. Though incidental in the process learning psychology, the fundamental knowledge about ICT is an added advantage for students as well as teachers.

ICT as a Medium of Knowledge Management

We are in an information society. This does not mean that there is lot of data in the society. It means we have easier access to information today than ever before. Data is just a number or figure. With context defined a data becomes meaningful information. Knowledge management is employing various strategies and practices combining information gathered by technology or any other means with our past experiences and insights to attain the goal. Modern technology provides for knowledge management also. Internet, email, social websites like blog, twitter etc., help us to manager our knowledge.

Conclusion

The above cited illustrations of uses of ICT in a Psychology class are not exhaustive. The scope is very wide. Everything depends on the ingenuity and interest of the teacher. Suitable conditions should be ensured in schools and teacher education Institutes to implement effectively ICT integration. Only then we can achieve our target in converting our classrooms to totally smart classes.

7

Traditional Classroom Vs Flipped Classroom

Introduction

Flipped classroom is a form of blended learning in which students learn new content online by watching video lectures, usually at home, and what used to be homework is done in class with teachers offering more personalized guidance and interaction with students, instead of lecturing. Teachers can deliver this instruction by recording and narrating screen casts of work they do on their computers, creating videos of themselves teaching, or creating video lessons from trusted Internet sites. Students can watch the videos or screen casts as many times as they need to, enabling them to be more productive learners in the classroom. Since direct instruction is delivered outside the group learning space, teachers can then use in-class time to actively engage students in the learning process and provide them with individualized support. The traditional pattern of teaching has been to assign students to read textbooks and work on problem sets outside school, while listening to lectures and taking tests in class. In flip teaching, the students first study the topic by themselves, typically using video lessons prepared by the teacher. Flipping changes teachers from "sage on the stage" to "guide on the side", allows them to work with individuals or groups of students throughout the session. Key elements of the flipped classroom are to provide a mechanism to assess students understanding. Provide an opportunity for students to gain first exposure prior to class, an incentive to students to prepare for the class and also promote in-class activities that focus on higher level cognitive activities. By providing an opportunity for students to use their new factual knowledge while they have access to immediate feedback from peers and instructor, the flipped classroom helps student learn to correct misconceptions and organize their new knowledge such that it is more accessible for future use.

More over the immediate feedback that occurs in the flipped classroom helps students recognize and think about their own growth in understanding. Originally developed in 2000 by Wes Baker at Cedarville University in Cedarville, Ohio, the flipped classroom model has gained widespread traction across the country as a means to integrate computer and online resources with day-to-day coursework. The flipped classroom is a pedagogical model in which the typical lecture and homework elements of a course are reversed. Short video lectures are viewed by students at home before the class session, while in-class time is devoted to exercises, projects, or discussions. The video lecture is often seen as the key ingredient in the flipped approach, such lectures being either created by the instructor and posted online or selected from an online repository. While a pre recorded lecture could certainly be a podcast or other audio format, the ease with which video can be accessed and viewed today has made it so ubiquitous that the flipped model has come to be identified with it.

Flipped Classroom

Flipped classroom is a form of blended learning in which students learn new content online by watching video lectures, usually at home, and what used to be homework is done in class with teachers offering more personalized guidance and interaction with students, instead of lecturing. This is also known as backwards classroom, reverse instruction, flipping the classroom and reverse teaching.

The flipped classroom approach has been used for years in some disciplines, notably within the humanities. The students gain first-exposure learning prior to class and focus on the processing part of learning like synthesizing, analyzing and problem- solving in the class. To ensure that students do the preparation necessary for productive class time, an assignment-based model in which students produce work prior to class. The students receive productive feedback on the students' work.

Traditional Vs Flipped Teaching

The traditional pattern of teaching has been to assign students to read textbooks and work on problem sets outside school, while listening to lectures and taking tests in class. In flip teaching, the students first study the topic by themselves, typically using video lessons prepared by the teacher. In class, students apply the knowledge by solving problems and doing practical work. Complementary techniques include differentiated instruction and project-based learning.

Flipped classrooms free class time for hands-on work. Students learn by doing and asking questions. Students can help each other, a process that benefits both the advanced and less advanced learners. Flipping also changes the allocation of teacher engages with the students who ask questions-but those who don't ask tend to need the most attention. We refer to 'silent failers,' said one teacher, claiming that flipping allows her to target those who need the most help rather than the most confident. Flipping changes teachers from "sage on the stage" to "guide on the side", allows them to work with individuals or groups of students throughout the session.

Significance of Flipped Classroom

1. In a traditional lecture, students often try to capture what is being said at the instant the speaker says it. They cannot stop to reflect upon what is being said, and they may miss significant points because they are trying to transcribe the instructor's words.

2. By contrast, the use of video and other pre- recorded media puts lectures under the control of the students: they can watch, rewind, and fast-forward as needed.

3. Lectures that can be viewed more than once may also help those for whom English is not their first language. Devoting class time to application of concepts might give instructors a better opportunity to detect errors in thinking, particularly those that are widespread in a class.

4. At the same time, collaborative projects can encourage social interaction among students, making it easier for them to learn from one another and for those of varying skill levels to support their peers.

5. Concept engagement takes place in the classroom with the help of the instructor. Educational Technology and activity learning are two key components of the flipped classroom model.

How Does It Work?

There is no single model for the flipped classroom the term is widely used to describe almost any class structure that provides pre-recorded lectures followed by in-class exercises. In one common model, students might view multiple lectures of five to seven minutes each. Online quizzes or activities can be interspersed to test what students have learned. Immediate quiz feedback and the ability to rerun lecture segments may help clarify points of confusion. Instructors might lead in class discussions or turn the classroom into a studio where students create, collaborate, and put into practice what they learned from the lectures they view outside class. As on-site experts, instructors suggest various approaches, clarify content, and monitor progress. They might organize students into an ad hoc workgroup to solve a problem that several are struggling to understand. Because this approach represents a comprehensive change in the class dynamic, some instructors have chosen to implement only a few elements of the flipped model or to flip only a few selected class sessions during a term.

Implications on Teaching and Learning

The flipped classroom constitutes a role change for instructors, who give up their front of the class position in favour of a more collaborative and cooperative contribution to the teaching process. There is a concomitant change in the role of students, many of who are used to being cast as passive participants in the education process, where instruction is served to them. Activities can be student-led, and communication among students can become the determining dynamic of a session devoted to learning through hands-on work. What the flip does particularly well is to bring about a distinctive shift in priorities from merely covering material to working toward mastery of it.

Key Elements of the Flipped Classroom

1. Provide an opportunity for students to gain first exposure prior to class.

2. Provide an incentive for students to prepare for the class.
3. Provide a mechanism to assess students understanding.
4. Provide in-class activities that focus on higher level cognitive activities.

Steps in Flipping the Classroom

1. Click on "Find and flip".
2. Find YouTube videos for your lessons.
3. Click to select that video then click on flip this video.
4. Listed/unlisted.
5. Title/description.
6. Customize your video lesson.
7. Click on finish flip when you are done you can also preview it before saving it.
8. Share
9. Lesson starts.

Advantages

1. Students take control of their learning.
2. The expectation of spending time doing homework should be clear
3. Student can develop foundation of factual knowledge.
4. Students can understand facts and ideas in the context of a conceptual framework.
5. They can enrich their knowledge in ways that facilitate retrieval and application.
6. saves time. Teacher may spend more time with students.

Conclusion

Meta-cognitive approach to instruction can help student learn to take control of their own learning by defining learning goals and monitoring their progress in achieving them. Although students thinking about the own learning is not an inherent part of the flipped classroom, the higher cognitive functions associated with class activity, accompanied by the ongoing peer/instructor interaction that typically accompanies them, can readily lead to the meta-cognition associated with deep learning.

References

1. Wesley, Baker.J (2000), The classroom flip: using web course management tools to become the guide by the side
2. Tucker, Bill (Winter 2012), "The Flipped Classroom", Education Next.
3. Pierce Richard, Fox Jeremy (20 Dec 2012), Vodcasts and active-learning exercises in a "flipped classroom" model of a renal pharmacotherapy module.
4. "Flipping the classroom", The Economist, 17 Sep 2011

8

Preparing the Academy of Today Learner

Introduction

Predicted to be America's first generation to exceed 100 million persons, the wave of Net Geners entering colleges and universities brings a blend of behaviors, attitudes, and expectations that creates opportunities—as well as challenges—for higher education. Opportunities arise from students' familiarity with technology, multitasking style, optimism, team orientation, diversity, and acceptance of authority. Challenges, on the other hand, include the shallowness of their reading and TV viewing habits, a comparative lack of critical thinking skills, naïve views on intellectual property and the authenticity of information found on the Internet, as well as high expectations combined with low satisfaction levels. Not surprisingly there is an increasing gap between most institutions' IT environments and the technologies the Net Gen uses. These factors lead, in turn, to the greatest challenge for higher education leaders, faculty, and staff—nearly all of whom belong to earlier generations: to understand the Net

Generation learner and through this understanding provide the learning environments, services, and facilities needed to help these students achieve their potential.

Most institutions profess intense interest in the academic, social, and personal needs of their students. Yet, generational differences are not often used to gain a better understanding of students' behaviors, attitudes, and expectations. Change and adaptation within the academy proceed at a slow, deliberate pace. Planning is complicated because personal characteristics are not homogeneous within generational groupings. Unfortunately, the generational literature fails to predict the characteristics of future generations. Institutional leaders need to find ways to think about generations in designing campus and individual student initiatives, as well as to discern trends that will allow future-directed planning.

Generations and Technology

The technologies available as a generation matures influence their behaviors, attitudes, and expectations. People internalize the technologies that shape information access and use, as well as the ways they communicate. Matures (born 1946–1964) were exposed to large vacuum-tube radios, mechanical calculators, 78 rpm records, dial telephones, and party lines. Baby Boomers grew up with transistor radios, mainframe computers, 33? and 45 rpm records, and the touchtone telephone. Gen-Xers matured in the era of CDs, personal computers, and electronic mail. For the Next Generation, the prevailing technologies are MP3s, cell phones, and PDAs; they communicate via instant messaging, text messaging, and blogs. For each successive generation "technology is only technology if it was invented after they were born."

Technology has experienced its own series of generations. In computing, the nexus has shifted from the mainframe to the minicomputer to the personal computer, and now to mobile devices. In line with Moore's Law, computing and communication devices have radically decreased in size and increased in performance. Connectivity has experienced a similar transition across generations, from no connectivity to proprietary device-to-device cabling, to globally interconnected local area networks, and now to wireless. Computers were initially developed as number crunching devices. The early emphasis on processing numbers, then words, has been joined by multimedia: graphics, images, video, sound, and interactive games. Prevalent among today's applications are interpersonal and group communication tools. The use of early computers was batch-processing-oriented and required programming skills and arcane commands. Today's graphical user interfaces and the Web make the operation of computers highly interactive and achievable by nearly anyone. The Internet has led to the kind of global village of information and communication.

Behaviors of the Net Generation are expressed through technologies to an extent not observed in previous generations. At one level, Net Geners are the beneficiaries of decades of technological development that preceded them; at another level, as students they use these technologies in new ways, and in so doing are redefining the landscape in higher education and perhaps beyond. To a great extent, the behaviors of the Net Gen are an enactment of the capabilities afforded by modern digital technologies.

According to a report from the Pew Internet & American Life Project, one in five of today's college students began using computers between the ages of 5 and 8; by the time they were 16 to 18, all of them used computers. Nationwide, nearly 90 percent of college students have gone online, compared with about 60 percent of the general population. Use of the Internet or campus networks is nearly universal in higher education. Eighty-five percent or more of college students own a computer, and nearly all of the rest have ready access to one. Sixty percent of college students regularly play computer or online games, and they are twice as likely to have downloaded music as the general population. The Net Generation students exhibit technology-related behaviors that may be unfamiliar to many in the academy: social networking, photo sharing, swarming, blogging, instant messaging, and text messaging. Four out of five students believe that Internet use has had a positive impact on their academic experience, and three out of four say they use the Internet for research more than they do the library.

Students are very familiar with the top online commercial sites such as Amazon. com and ambercrombie.com; they hold these sites to be the standard against which they judge colleges' online services. And, of all of the generational groups, the Net Generation is least satisfied with their higher education experience. Net Geners have access to affordable multifunctional devices (for example, cell phones equipped with digital cameras and Web browsers that can play digital audio and video recordings, as well as send and receive e-mail and text messages) that readily support their interpersonal communication needs and multitasking behaviors. Between classes, students bustle about with cell phones attached to their ears. Silberman described the prevalence of cell phones among Net Geners in Finland, and how cell phones' voice and short messaging capabilities allow them to move in synchronization "like schools of fish ... on currents of whim." This behavior has since become well established in America, where it is known as social swarming or smart mobs.

Emerging Patterns

The mobility enabled by wireless communication, combined with an expanding class of wireless-equipped portable computers and PDAs, is leading to new instructional and social patterns. No longer do students need to go to a specific place, or even be seated, to use a computer. An array of multifunctional PDAs capable of wireless communication is allowing such devices to follow their users wherever they go, serving as "prosthetics for information, memory, or creativity." This is challenging the very definition of learning spaces because learning can now occur both in and out of the classroom, in both formal and informal settings, and by lone scholars or among groups. Net Gen students not only use technology heavily, they also trust it implicitly. They are as likely to get their news online as from a newspaper and conduct research through Google as visit a library. Their belief that anything accessible online should be free leads many to download or share music, movies, or software they have not purchased. The extent of this activity has surprised many institutions; campus networks often became saturated when students returned to school in the fall. In some cases this is followed by copyright violation notices from organizations such as the Recording Industry Association of America. The interactive and exploratory way the Net Generation uses technology is also a break with the past. The Net Gen approaches computers and other technologies as environments for communication, socialization, learning, and game playing, not as machines to be programmed. To be sure, today's students are avid users of Web, e-mail, telephones, and other IT resources; however, their rapid adoption of instant messaging, cell phones, blogs, wikis, social networking Web sites, and other resources that are not generally part of the core campus infrastructure leads to a host of new concerns. There is increased potential for incompatibilities between the technologies adopted by students and campus standards. The real opportunity lies in observing and talking to today's students to learn more about how they conceptualize and use these new tools. With this knowledge institutions can create contexts for technology use that enhance learning, improve student services, and enrich students' social lives.

Assessing the Generations in Online Learning

The Research Initiative for Teaching Effectiveness (RITE) at the University of Central Florida (UCF) regularly conducts formative and summative surveys of students' online learning experiences. These data become transformative because they are instrumental in modifying the organization, structure, and processes of our distributed learning initiative. We believe that both qualitative and quantitative research yield a more valid assessment of students in the online learning environment. When we ask respondents to complete objective statements followed by a reflective narrative, we obtain a more authentic characterization of their attitudes, beliefs, and behaviors. In the latest survey conducted at UCF, students used a series of 5-point Likert-scale questions to evaluate their online learning experience around two components previously identified through extensive numerical work. The first domain—learning engagement—encompassed six items where students indicated there:

1. Overall satisfaction with online learning
2. Ability to integrate technology into their education
3. Ability to control their own learning
4. Ability to study efficiently
5. Ability to meet their educational objectives
6. Willingness to take another online course
7. The second domain—interaction value—asked students to evaluate their online learning experience in regard to:
8. Ease of interaction
9. Amount of interaction with students
10. Quality of interaction with students
11. Amount of interaction with the instructor
12. Quality of interaction with the instructor

Excellent Teaching

From our exploration of generational issues, an important

question evolved: Can students distinguish characterizations of excellent teachers independent of generation, learning style, course modality, and technological sophistication? Data collected at UCF, with more than half a million student responses, suggest an answer. We have identified six characteristics that students attribute to the best faculty—characteristics that are independent of age, gender, and academic achievement. Interestingly, these characteristics correspond to the seven principles of good practice in undergraduate education and to the national study of student engagement. Although students' behaviors, attitudes, and expectations are generally shaped by their generation, what constitutes good teaching appears to be universal across these generations. Students believe that excellent instructors:

1. Facilitate student learning
2. Communicate ideas and information effectively
3. Demonstrate genuine interest in student learning
4. Organize their courses effectively
5. Show respect and concern for their students
6. Assess student progress fairly and effectively

This seemingly paradoxical way in which students determine teaching excellence through the lens of their instructors clarifies how universities must accommodate students' needs, realizing that these needs are universal, yet greatly mediated by the Net Generation.

Conclusion

The Net Generation possesses sophisticated technological adaptability and a remarkable capacity to incorporate multitasking into day-to-day academic activities. However, there is also a growing discrepancy between institutional infrastructure and these students' personalized facility with information. Freeland described a corresponding trend emerging in higher education that he called practice-oriented education—the combination of liberal and professional studies. He foreshadowed the students' tendency to learn through bricolage and the university's reticence to respond: "After 1945 it [the academy] became steadily more open... [but] as its clientele became more 'modern,' higher education became more traditional." As we move into the next decades, the resolution of that polarization compels colleges and universities to examine, and perhaps redesign, their strategic direction. Possibly, by studying how students interacted (politically, economically, culturally, socially, and technologically) with institutions' instructional climate in the past. From an instructional design perspective, we realize that knowing our students gives us many more options for engaging them in the learning process. The audacity with which the Net generation has burst on the academic scene has accelerated our need to understand its learning characteristics. A conundrum accompanies that solution, however: adaptation for the present generation may not be adequate for the next.

References

1. Neil Howe and William Strauss, Millennial Rising: The Next Greatest Generation (New York: Vintage Books, 2000).
2. Alan Kay quoted in Marc Prensky, Digital Game-Based Learning (New York: McGraw- Hill, 2000), p. 38.
3. Marshall McLuhan and Bruce R. Powers, The Global Village: Transformations in World Life and Media in the 21st Century (New York: Oxford University Press, 1999).
4. Steve Jones et al., "The Internet Goes to College: How Students Are Living in the Future with Today's Technology" (Washington, D.C.: Pew Internet & American Life Project, September 15, 2002), <http://www.pewinternet.org/reports/toc.asp?Report=71>.

9

Effectiveness of Edu-digital Skill Among Higher Secondary Students

Introduction

The end of the 20th Century and beginning of the 21st Century witnessed very exciting changes, one of them being in the field of Information and Communication Technology. Educators have begin to realize that in the fast changing world of today, the students have to be prepared to cope intelligently with the social, economic and technological changes. The educational environment is changing rapidly as a consequence of ICT and will continue to change. Information and Communication Technologies (ICT) are electronic and/or computerized devices and associated human interactive materials that enable the user to employ them for a wide range of teaching and learning processes in addition to personal use. Around the world, educational systems are under increasing pressure to use the new information and communication technologies to teach students the knowledge and skills they need in the 21st Century. With the emerging new technologies, the teaching profession is evolving from an emphasis on teacher-centered, lecture-based instruction to student-centered, interactive learning environments. The present study aims to find out the effectiveness of edu-digital skill among higher secondary students in Coimbatore District. A samples of 100 higher secondary students selected randomly were studied. A questionnaire method of survey was used to find out the effectiveness of edu-digital skill higher secondary students. The data were collected by using questionnaire as an instrument. Primary data were collected by conducting direct structured interview using questionnaire. All the respondents were asked the same questions in the same fashion and they were informed the purpose of study. t-test, Regression and correlation analysis were applied to test the hypotheses. The findings and observations are the result and outcome of the interpretations made during the study of analysis. The result found that edu-digital skills are positively correlated with higher secondary students.

Education, the foremost weapon for social reform, is now under the forces of change. Newly formed branches of knowledge and techniques of education facilitate the physical, mental and emotional development of the learners. Schools have an unavoidable role in acquainting the students with the nature of changing field of education and in making necessary changes in the instructional techniques. In the modern world of technological innovations, all educational institutions are trying to improve their quality in terms of facilities and academic outputs.

Scientific knowledge is exploding every day. Knowledge available to mankind today is emerging in the form of science and technology. There is no limit or end to the accumulation of scientific knowledge. It also satisfies the intellectual thirst of human beings. Science education is a bridge between science and education, using psychology. It links the most powerful concepts of science to the growing minds of children through active experimental pedagogy. Science education plays a prominent role in Indian educational system. It has, as its objective, the aim of providing individual learners a firm grasp of the concepts and processes of science as also to impart the ability to use scientific method of problem-solving. As a result of it, every aspect of human civilization has been influenced to a very great extent.

The present world is the world of science and technology. Science is the most inexhaustible storehouse of knowledge. Continuous advances in scientific and technological research have led to the growth and greater application of science in contemporary society. The purpose of science education is to give individuals a firm grasps of the concepts and processes of science and to develop scientific attitude, scientific reasoning, problem solving ability and scientific temper and to impart them the ability to use the scientific method to other situations in life. Hence science education has been included in school curriculum at all levels. It is however necessary that science teaching be impressive so as to inculcate its values in young minds.

The increasing importance of informatics in day-to-day life has resulted in the emergence of computers in education at the international level. The worldwide recognition gained for the importance of computers has compelled educationists to revise the existing curricula to include informatics components. Even the developing countries have realized that unless they invest heavily in computer education, they will be left behind in the informatics revolution. Computers are being used in education to prepare the children for the informatics future by training them in programming and related skills for work in the informatics industry. They are also being used as educational aids to improve children's skills in academic subjects at all levels of education. Introduction of computers in education has brought out changes in the content and methods of education. However, lack of resources remains one of the main obstacles to the introduction and development of informatics in education in a large way in developing countries.

The most striking innovation in the field of educational technology is the use of computers. Computer is included in the hardware approach of educational technology. It is one of the machines of automation in teaching and learning and is used for presenting individualized instruction. The main objective of teaching through computer is to provide the needed flexibility for individualizing the educational process. It meets the specific needs of the student in a way in which is almost impossible to do in a face-to face student-teacher relationship.

Computers should have a major role in the teaching-learning process. Computers have become an essential class room tool for the acquisition, analysis, presentation, and communication of data in ways that allow students to become active participants in research and learning. The computers offer students very important resources for learning concepts through simulations, graphics, sound, data manipulation and model building. Computers can improve scientific learning and facilitate communication of ideas and concepts.

There are three roles for computer in education. First, it functions as a tutor for students by presenting material, evaluating responses, and depending on the basis of the evaluation, deciding what to present next. Second, it is a tool that helps students perform calculations, analyze data, keep records, or write papers. Third, it functions as tutee by having told what to do through programming.

A computer program can be designed to create models for experimental purpose. Students, that particularly in higher education, have the benefits of using computer as a computational tool. They learn a programming language and write a program to solve some of their course work problems treating the computer as an aid in much the same way as a slide rule or a set of mathematical tables. Computers are capable of giving almost instant feedback, tirelessly, no matter how many learners 'get it wrong' and it is equally well known that human tutors have limited value when it comes to learners repeatedly getting things wrong.

Review of Literature

Dalacosta et al. (2009) developed and studied the effectiveness of Multimedia application with animated cartoons in teaching science in elementary education. The results of the study provide evidence that the use of animated cartoons significantly increases the young students' knowledge and understanding of specific science concepts, which are normally difficult to comprehend and often cause misconceptions to them.

Jian Hu et al. (2009) investigated the effects of introducing a software program, named the Dental 3D Multimedia System (D3DM), into the education of a group of junior dental students in their preclinical practice. One group received their training program in the traditional way, unassisted by 3D technology. The second group received their training program in the traditional manner, but also used the D3DM to supplement their education. The results showed that the D3DM-assisted group achieved higher scores and also indicated that the usage of 3D multimedia PC software had a positive impact on several aspects of subjects' performance.

Kanmani and Radha (2009) studied the Effectiveness of CAI package in basic electronics teaching. There was a significant difference between the control and the experimental group students in attainment of knowledge level, understanding level, and application level objective in the gain scores. Hence, the experimental group students were better than the control group students in attainment of knowledge level, understanding level, and application level objective in the gain scores. It was inferred from the finding that the experimental treatment is effective to the students.

Korakakis et al. (2009) made a study on the "3D visualization types in multimedia applications for science learning for 8th grade students in Greece". The aim of the study was to determine whether the use of specific types of visualization (3D illustration, 3D animation, and interactive 3D animation) combined with narration and text, contributes to the learning process in science courses. The results indicated that multimedia applications with interactive 3D animations as well as with 3D animations do in fact increase the interest of students and make the material more appealing to them.

She, Hsiao-Ching and Chen, Yi-Zen (2009) examined how middle school students constructed their understanding of the mitosis and meiosis processes at a molecular level through multimedia learning materials presented in different interaction and sensory modality modes. The dependent variables included subjects' pre-test, post-test, and retention-test scores, showing their understanding of mitosis and meiosis process at molecular level. The results of the study showed that the group which used multimedia learning material has a greater amount of visual attention and consistent with their long term retained learning than the group which did not use the same. This study adds empirical evidence of a direct correlation between the length of eye fixation behavior and the depth of learning. Moreover, it provides insight into the multimedia effect on students' cognitive process through the use of eye fixation behavior evidence.

Anboucarassy (2010) studied the effectiveness of Multimedia in Teaching Biological Science to IX Standard students. The results of the study revealed that experiment group performed better than the control group due to the exposure of multimedia based learning. Thus multimedia helps the students to sustain their interest and also their retention power compared to the traditional method of teaching. The constant use of multimedia will make students understand more and achieve more in their academic achievement. Hence it was concluded that the multimedia approach is considered to be one of the best techniques for biology teaching at IX standard level.

Ponraj and Sivakumar (2010) studied the effectiveness of Computer-Assisted Instruction in Teaching Zoology in Relation to Learners' Personality. The major findings of the study indicated that achievement scores of experimental group students were higher than the control group students after the treatment.

Yusuf, Mudasiru and Afolabi, Adedeji (2010) investigated the effects of computer assisted instruction (CAI) on secondary school students' performance in biology. The findings of the study showed that the performance of students exposed to CAI either individually or cooperatively were better than their counterparts exposed to the conventional classroom instruction. Based on the research findings recommendations were made on the need to develop relevant CAI packages for teaching biology in Nigerian secondary schools.

Objectives

1. To know the edu-digital skill among higher secondary students in Coimbatore district.
2. To find out the effectiveness of Multimedia Programme in teaching among higher secondary students.

Methodology

Research may be termed as a systemic inquiry of verified knowledge; it is an organized deliberate effort to collect information, to analyze it, to put it together and finally to evaluate it. This research paper on methodology describes elaborately, the sample that was chosen, research design, objectives of the study, data collection, statistical techniques used for data and analysis.

Population

Population selected for this study was 100 higher secondary students in a selected school at Coimbatore District.

Attitude Scale Towards Multimedia Programme

The attitude scale was used to measure the level of attitude towards Multimedia programme. The scale was constructed and validated by the investigator.

The attitude scale towards multimedia programme, consisting of 40 items, was designed by the investigator and was given to experienced teachers who were handling Computer Science in higher secondary schools, professors of Computer Science and Education and Educational psychologists. On the basis of the suggestions of above experts, some items were restructured and some were eliminated. Finally 25 items were selected for this test. The scale for measuring the higher secondary student's attitude towards multimedia programme in the study is of the Liker type. This scale has as many as 25 statements of which 20 are favourable towards multimedia programme and the remaining are unfavourable towards it.

Scoring

In the Likert type of scale, against each statement, five alternatives namely "Strongly agree", "Agree", "Undecided", "Disagree", and "Strongly disagree" are given. The subjects have to indicate their choice by putting a tick-mark (") under one of the five columns against each statement.

For favourable statement weightage of 4,3,2,1 and 0 were given from strongly agree to strongly disagree in that order. For unfavourable statements the scoring was reversed. Thus the strongly agree response will get 0 and the strongly disagree response will get 4. Here the weightage of 0,1,2,3 and 4 were given from strongly agree to the strongly disagree in that order.

Thus the score value lies between 0-100. The content validity of the tool was established based on the opinion given by the experts. The reliability of the tool was established by Split-Half method. It was found to be 0.83 which was significant.

Data Collection

Primary data, required for the present research work were collected by conducting direct interviews using questionnaire. All the respondents were given sufficient information about the Project work. These respondents were provided with the same questionnaires. They were also informed that they have to answer in the same fashion.

Hypothesis

There is no significant difference between the pre and post test mean scores of experimental group students in their attitude towards multimedia programme.

Administration of retention test

The Attitude Scale towards Multimedia Programme was constructed and validated by the investigator and was administered to the subjects of the experimental group. The pre test scores on attitude towards multimedia programme were collected. Thus pre test and post test scores on attitude towards multimedia programme were computed for analysis.

Analysis and Interpretation

To find out the significance of the difference between the pre and post test mean scores of experimental group students in their attitude towards multimedia programme the ‘t’ test was used.

Table 1 : Distribution of 't' value between the pre and post test mean scores of experimental group students in their attitude towards multimedia programme

Group	N	Mean	S.D	't' value	Level of Significant
Pre test	50	42.08	10.42	24.47	p<0.05
Post test	50	93.58	2.57		

There is no significant difference between the pre and post test mean scores of experimental group students in their attitude towards multimedia programme.

The obtained 't' value is statistically significant since it is greater than the table 't' value 1.96 at 0.05 level of significance. Hence the null hypothesis is rejected. It shows that there is significant difference between the pre and post test mean scores of experimental group students in their attitude towards multimedia programme. It is therefore concluded that the experimental group students show more favourable attitude towards multimedia programme in the post test than the pre test.

Table 2 : Showing the Stepwise regression analysis predicting factors influencing effectiveness of edu-digital skill among higher secondary students and demographic variables

Sl.No	Step/Source	Unstandardized Coefficients Beta	Std. Error	Standardized Coefficients Beta Beta	Step t	P
1.	Gender	1.144	0.156	0.242	7.324	0.01
2.	Father education	1.254	0.359	0.163	3.495	0.01
3.	Mother education	2.615	0.462	0.361	5.661	0.01
4.	Monthly Income	2.175	0.402	0.280	5.410	0.01
5.	Father Occupation	1.022	0.513	0.137	1.992	0.01

* P < 0.01

Five variables viz Gender, Father Education, Mother Education, Monthly income and Father Occupation have significantly contributed for predicting the factors influencing effectiveness of edu-digital skill among higher secondary. The first variable Gender seems to be 7.324, Father Education seems to be 3.495, Mother education seems to be 5.661, Monthly income seems to be 5.410 and Father Occupation seems to be 1.992. The predictive value of these variables separately is 0.01.

Table 3 : Showing the correlation between the effectiveness of edu-digital skill among higher secondary students and demographic variables

Factors	Effectiveness of edu-digital skill among higher secondary students
Gender	0.920**
Father education	0.849**
Mother education	0.914**
Monthly Income	0.880**
Father Occupation	0.855**

* Significant at 0.01 level

Effectiveness of edu-digital skill among higher secondary students is positively and significantly related to Gender (0.920), Father education (0.849), Mother education (0.914), monthly income (0.880) and Father Occupation (0.855). So, the direct relationship between the effectiveness of edu-digital skill among higher secondary students and selected demographic variables.

Conclusion

Computer and multimedia technology for education offers a number of benefits. They allow the teacher to structure and present the information with varying special effects to the students. They can also be used for the storage of audio-visual information of various types. Multimedia programmes provide a lot of benefits. The benefits for learners include flexibility of scheduled instruction at a location convenient to learners, reduced student time, assured progress in skill development, increased achievement and increased retention and continuous report to the learners of progress and accomplishments, specified performance criteria, good response and feedback. The application of multimedia programme would definitely create a good learning environment in classroom, sustaining attention and motivating the students to learn effectively. The application of multimedia may create a congenial learning climate in schools and can bring real life situations.

The investigator has chosen the topic for the present study in order to address the problem faced by teachers, teaching science, to foster involvement in new teaching approaches, to get a feeling of satisfaction through learning in the classroom, to create joyful learning environment and to stimulate active information processing for effective learning,

In a vast country like India, enormous work is now being done in the field of education, but it is still not possible to equip each and every school with all the facilities for teaching science. Secondary schools need high quality teaching aids. Multimedia, as a teaching aid, is very much effective with colour, sound and graphics, which are found in the audio, video movie media. Any diagram can be explained in detail with 3D effects, which helps the students understand clearly. The students can get a live vision of life's aspects and scientific factors. Multimedia includes use of computer.

References

1. Anboucarassy, B. (2010). Effectiveness of Multimedia in Teaching Biological Science to IX Standard students. EDUTRACKS, 9(5): 37-38.

2. Dalacosta, K., Kamariotaki-Paparrigopoulou, M., Palyvos, J.A., & Spyrellis, N. (2009). Multimedia application with animated cartoons for teaching science in elementary education. Computers & Education, 52(4): 741-748. Retrieved March 20, 2010 http://www.linkinghub.elsevier.com/retrieve/pii/S0360131508001905

3. Jian Hu, Hao Yu, Jun Shao, Zhiyong Li, Jiawei Wang & Yining Wang (2009). Effects of dental 3D multimedia system on the performance of junior dental students in preclinical practice: a report from China. Advances in Health Sciences Education, 14(1): 123 – 133. Retrieved March 20, 2010 http://www.springerlink.com/content/c0n8075m367131x1/

4. Kanmani, M., & Radha, M. (2009). "Effectiveness of CAI package in basic electronics teaching", Journal of All India Association for Educational Research, 21(1): 47-50.

5. Korakakis, G., Pavlatou, E.A., Palyvos, J. A., & Spyrellis N. (2009). 3D visualization types in multimedia applications for science learning: A case study for 8th grade students in Greece. Computers & Education, 52(2): 390-401. Retrieved March 21, 2010 http://portal.acm.org/citation.cfm?id=1480558

6. Ponraj, P., & Sivakumar, R. (2010). Computer-Assisted Instruction in Zoology in Relation to Learners' Personality. EDUTRACKS, 9(6): 34-37.

7. Yusuf, Mudasiru O., & Afolabi, Adedeji O. (2010). Effects of Computer Assisted instruction (CAI) on Secondary School students' performance in biology. TOJET: The Turkish Online Journal of Educational Technology, 9(1): 62-69. Retrieved March 21, 2010

10

Integrating ICT in Education

Introduction

Information Communication Technologies are the power that has changed many aspects of the lives. The education is a socially oriented activity. It plays vital role in building the society. The quality education traditionally is associated with strong teachers having high degrees. Using ICTs in education it moved to more student –centered learning As world is moving rapidly towards digital information, the role of ICTs in education becoming more and more important and this importance will continue to grow and develop in 21st century. This paper highlights various impacts of ICT on contemporary education and also discusses the major barriers faced in the process of integration. The paper argues the role of ICT in transforming teacher-centered learning to competency based learning. It also explores some recommendations to overcome those barriers.

Information and Communication Technologies (ICT) that are becoming increasingly pervasive in societies around the world are also reaching schools. With numerous global advancements in ICT it is essential that educators have a thorough working knowledge of these media and their influence on the performance and engagement of their students. There is no firm agreement on the definition of ICT, as these technologies evolve almost daily. The 21st Century Society is an entrepreneurial Society- A century of knowledge and century of mind. Knowledge explosion, communication revolution, technology advancement, application of science to all aspects of life and above all rising aspirations of the society are the hallmarks of this century.

Use of ICT in Teaching Learning

Teaching at School, mostly, concentrates on giving information which is not the sole objective of Teaching. Along with giving information, the other objectives are:

1. developing understanding and application of the concepts
2. development of reasoning power and decision making ability
3. improving comprehension, speed and vocabulary
4. developing self-concept and study habits
5. developing proper study habits
6. developing tolerance, risk taking capacity, scientific temper, etc.

In India with the present infrastructure, class size, availability of teachers, quality of teachers, training of teachers, etc., it is difficult to realize all the objectives. As the objectives are multi-dimensional in nature, multiple methods should be used in an integrated fashion in teaching learning. At present ICT may be of some use. It is a well known fact that not a single teacher is capable of giving up to date and complete information in his own subject. The ICT can fill this gap because it can provide access to different sources of information.

Use of ICT in Diagnostic Testing and Remedial Teaching

Computer Based Diagnostic Tests will help the teachers as well as students in identifying the gray area of each and every student. This can be put on the website of the school and the student can access to it from home also. The student can learn the topic and can take the test to find exactly what he has not understood. The teacher cannot do this manually. The student progress can be monitored and his performance can be improved. This will develop confidence in students and may change their attitude towards the subject. It may also help in reducing the suicidal tendency among students. Students may start enjoying learning. The Remedial Teaching can be done by the teacher if some common mistakes are identified. It may not be feasible to organize remedial programme for individual students.

Use of ICT in Evaluation

At present the paper pencil tests are conducted for evaluating the academic performance of students. The content coverage is poor and students cannot use them on their own. These tests are evaluated by the teachers and they may not give feedback immediately to each and every student. It may be due to this that students are unable to know their weakness and do not make any attempt to improve upon them. The ICT can be made use in the evaluation. The test can be used by individual student to evaluate his learning. The student can instantaneously get the feedback about the status of his understanding. It goes a long way in improving the learning and teacher has no role to play in it. Such tests can be uploaded on the website for wider use. The students from other institutes can also make use of it. Not only the students even the teachers can also use it to assess their own understanding of the subject.

Use f ICT in Psychological Testing

The psychological testing is laborious and involves money and time. This is the age of digital technology. It can be used to digitalize all the psychological tests including the scoring and evaluation. The same may be available on the website and students and teachers can use them whenever required. Even student can use it individually and can share the result with the teacher who can help the student to improve his academic performance. The digitalized psychological tests will be easy to use and economical also.

Use of ICT in Developing Virtual Laboratory

If the Virtual Laboratory is developed, it can provide lots of freedom to students. The students can manipulate any attribute or variable related to the experiment and can see how it affects the outcome. The Virtual Laboratory can be developed using ICT. It may be made available at the door step of each and every student by uploading it on the Website.

Use of ICT in Online Tutoring

Online tutoring makes the students stay at their home. They logs in to their tutor through the use of Internet and software. It will make the academic life of many students easy. This is also how the knowledge power available in India can be made use of other countries.

Use of ICT in Developing Instructional Material

There are many teachers who are well known for their specialties in the subject. Their lectures should be digitalized and made available to all the users. It will enhance the quality of instruction in the classrooms. The teacher can use them in the classrooms and can organize discussion after it wherein the new points can be added both by the teacher as well as students. It will make the teaching effective, participatory and enjoyable.

Barriers of Integration of ICT in Education

Teacher Level Barriers

1. Several researchers indicate that one barrier that prevents teachers from using ICT in their teaching is lack of confidence. Beggs (2000) asserted the teachers "fear of failure" caused a lack of confidence.
2. The second teacher level barrier is the lack of knowledge and skills to use computers in their teaching process.
3. Resistance to change and negative attitudes towards ICT is one of the important teacher related barriers.

School Level Barriers

1. Lack of time for teachers in many aspects of their work as it affects their ability to complete tasks, with some of the teachers specifically stating which aspects of ICT require more time.
2. There are not enough training opportunities for teachers in the use of ICT's in a classroom environment. Lack of opportunities for professional development obstructed them from integrating technology in certain subjects such as science and maths.
3. Lack of access to resources in schools discourages teachers from integrating new technologies into education.
4. Lack of Technical support was found to be a major barrier for teachers in the integration of ICT in education.

Government commitment to the use of ICT in schools in india

India has one of the lowest "pupils to computers ratio" in the world. Much investment is required for the provision of dedicated ICT rooms where pupils would gain 'hands on' experience of using Excel, Word, PowerPoint, Video conference, Internet etc. The poor investment by the government to the schools in integrating the ICT is seen in India.

Barriers in the Process of Preparing the Teachers

In the majority of teacher education programme offered in India, the syllabi exhibit less weight to practical than theoretical aspects. Since the nature of ICT subjects is more practical and application-oriented, there needs to be more practical than theoretical input in our curriculum related to teacher education.

Recommendations in the Integrating the ICT in education

Recognizing the importance of ICT in education, ICT has been included as a core course at the B.Ed level in the colleges. Teacher Trainees need more structured support of ICT development from their educational institutions. There must be congruence between the school curriculum and teacher training curriculum. Otherwise, teachers are not ready to utilize their knowledge to effectively design teaching/learning processes, project work, and assignments. In addition to offering ICT as a compulsory and special course, integrated approaches need to be studied along with methods courses. This will help pupil-teachers to develop the concept of 'techno pedagogy' to a greater extent. Enrolling the teachers for online professionally development courses. There are many websites offering free training modules. Enrolling for the best commercially available ICT training programs. The teachers should attend the ICT related courses, seminars, conferences and workshop for their professional development.

The schools which are committed to preparing students for the future information society empower them to become more active learners constructing their own learning situations. In this learning mode, ICT applications become vital and more user-oriented. In this case the physical environment is made more suitable for learning individually and in small groups. Government cooperation is necessary for implementing the ICT programmes to have substantial impact and be sustainable. The active participation of the Government is essential to ensure the sector-wise introduction of ICT. Prioritizing and Planning Access to Remote Areas and Special consideration should be given to ICT connectivity and accessibility for educational purposes.

Conclusion

The role of ICTs in the education is recurring and unavoidable. Rapid changes in the technologies are indicating that the role of ICT in future will grow tremendously in education. ICT also focuses modification of the role of teachers. In addition to classroom teaching, they will have other skills and responsibilities. Teachers will act as virtual guides for students who use electronic media. Ultimately, the use of ICT will enhance the learning experiences of students. Also it helps them to think independently and communicate creatively. It also helps students for building successful careers and lives, in an increasingly technological world.

11

Blended Learning Programs

Introduction

This Article highlights the Models of Blended learning programs. The majority of blended-learning programs resemble one of four models: Rotation, Flex, A La Carte, and Enriched Virtual. The Rotation model includes four sub-models: Station Rotation, Lab Rotation, Flipped Classroom, and Individual Rotation.

Blended learning is a formal education program in which a student learns at least in part through online delivery of content and instruction with some element of student control over time, place, path or pace. It is the face-to-face classroom methods that are combined with computer-mediated activities. Blended learning occurs within a face-to-face class that happens at a specific place and time. Blended learning combines the support of classroom learning with the flexibility of e-learning. Blended learning is a term increasingly used to describe the way e-learning being combined with traditional classroom methods and independent study to create a new, hybrid teaching methodology.

A program in which within a given course or subject (e.g., math), students rotate between learning modalities, at least one of which is online learning. Other modalities might include activities such as small-group or full-class instruction, group projects, individual tutoring, and pencil-and-paper assignments.

a. Station Rotation (also referred to as Classroom Rotation or In-Class Rotation) — A Rotation-model implementation in which within a given course or subject (e.g., math), students rotate on a fixed schedule or at the teacher's discretion among classroom-based learning modalities. The rotation includes at least one station for online learning. Other stations might include activities such as small-group or full-class instruction, group projects, individual tutoring, and pencil-and-paper assignments. Some implementations involve the entire class alternating among activities together, whereas others divide the class into small-group or one-by-one rotations. The Station Rotation model differs from the Individual Rotation model because students rotate through all of the stations, not only those on their custom schedules.

b. Lab Rotation — A Rotation-model implementation in which within a given course or subject (e.g., math), students rotates on a fixed schedule or at the teacher's discretion among locations on the brick-and-mortar campus. At least one is a learning lab for predominantly online learning, and the other(s) are classroom(s) for other learning modalities. The Lab Rotation model differs from the Station Rotation model because students rotate among locations on the campus instead of staying in one classroom for the blended course or subject.

c. Flipped Classroom — A Rotation-model implementation in which within a given course or subject (e.g.. math), students rotate on a fixed schedule between face-to-face teacher-guided practice (or projects) on campus during the standard school day and online delivery of content and instruction of the same subject from a remote location (often home) after school. The primary delivery of content and instruction is online, which differentiates a Flipped Classroom from students who are merely doing homework practice online at night. The Flipped Classroom model accords with the idea that blended learning includes some element of student control over time, place, path, and/or pace because the model allows students to choose the location where they receive content and instruction online.

d. Individual Rotation — A Rotation-model implementation in which within a given course or subject (e.g., math), students rotate on an individually customized, fixed schedule among learning modalities, at least one of which is online learning. An algorithm or teacher sets individual student schedules. The Individual Rotation model differs from the other Rotation models because students do not necessarily rotate to each available station or modality.

2. Flex model

A program in which the online learning is the backbone of student learning, even if it directs students to offline activities at times. Students move on an individually customized, fluid schedule among learning modalities, and the teacher of record is on-site. The teacher-of-record or other adults provide face-to-face support on a flexible and adaptive as-needed basis through activities such as small-group instruction, group projects, and individual tutoring. Some implementations have substantial face-to-face support, and others have minimal (e.g., some Flex models may have face-to-face certified teachers who supplement the online learning on a daily basis, whereas others may provide little face-to-face enrichment; others may have different staffing combinations; these are useful modifiers to describe a particular Flex model).

3. A La Carte model (formerly Self-Blend model)

A program in which students take one or more courses entirely online with an online teacher of record and at the same time continue to have brick-and-mortar educational experiences. Students may take the online courses either on the brick-and-mortar campus or off-site. This differs from full-time online learning and the Enriched Virtual model because it is not a whole-school experience.

4. Enriched Virtual model

A whole-school experience in which within each course (e.g., math), students divide their time between attending a brick-and-mortar campus and learning remotely using online delivery of content and instruction. Many Enriched Virtual programs began as full-time online schools and then developed blended programs to provide students with brick-and-mortar school experiences. The Enriched Virtual model differs from the Flipped Classroom because in Enriched Virtual programs, students seldom attend the brick-and-mortar campus every weekday. It differs from the A La Carte model because it is a whole-school experience, not a course-by-course model.

Conclusion

Blended learning use as the tools of the provincial learning management system to teach and support learning in a face-to-face class. Through blended learning, students can access high-quality course materials, course calendars, and assignments during and outside school hours. Students can also take part in face-to-face lessons and communicate with their teacher and classmates using a suite of secure online tools inside the password-protected learning management system.

References

1. Bonk, C.J., & Graham, C.R. (2006). The handbook of blended learning environments: Global perspectives, local designs. San Francisco: Jossey Bass/Pfeiffer. p.5.
2. Garrison, D. R., & Kanuka, H. (2004). Blended learning: Uncovering its transformative potential in higher education. The Internet and Higher Education, 7, 95–105.
3. Harel Caperton, Idit. (2012) Learning to Make Games for Impact. The Journal of Media Literacy, 59(1), 28-38.
4. Staker and Horn (2012) "Blended Learning" (PDF). Retrieved 2013-10-24.

12

The Impact of Science and Technology Among Students

Introduction

There is a tremendous revolution in science and technology. Information in communication technologies has a deep cultural revolution changing. There is a need to make a realistic assessment of what technology cannot do to reach a plateau of productivity when the technology consistently delivers to realistic goals.

Digital skill is a vast technique used by all people. Educational technology and mobile learning, multi- media learning are all digital skill. Science is a boon. Man has discovered many wonderful things from the treasure of developing every day. It has made our life easier, happier and more secure. Science and technology has conquered time and space. It has made very good communication and made the transport easier. With the help of science and technology, modern medicine and medical treatments, the doctors save the life of sick people from the jaws of death. Many organs are now transplanted. It is used in the field of agriculture. The impact of science and technology among students in the field is both good and bad.

Science laboratory, space centre ISRO are taken in the highest form. Television, telecommunication, type- recorder, films, LCD projectors, digital and white board, e- learning, e-teaching, teleconferencing, teaching machine cell phones such as all types of multimedia are boons to us. But the students are affected by this because of misusing. So they blamed science. We cannot blame science. It is a wonderful boon.

Digital skill in website

By the wrong use of face book, web site, web-camera, especially cell phones, net connection, lab top etc. Science and technology become down. But once for all where we use science and technology in proper, correct and perfect way it is a boon to us otherwise it is curse and demon to us.

A secondary Information and Communication Technology curriculum should contribute to the building up of teams of professionals with these new competencies. The use of Information and Communication Technology cuts across all aspects of economic and social life. Technological developments in Information and Communication Technology are very rapid. Technology quickly becomes obsolete requiring new skills and knowledge to be mastered frequently. Adaptation is only possible when based on a sound understanding of the principles and concepts of Information and Communication Technology.

Review of Literature

Lei, Jing (2010) studied on Quantity versus Quality: A New Approach to Examine the Relationship between Technology Use and Student Outcomes. It is found that that to examine the relationship between technology use and student outcomes, the quality of technology use—how, and what, technology is used—is a more significant factor than the quantity of technology use—how much technology is used. This argument was exemplified by an empirical study that used both angles to examine the association between technology use and student outcomes. When only the quantity of technology use was examined, no significant association was observed. However, when the quality of technology was examined by investigating the specific types of technology uses, a significant association was identified between technology use and all student outcomes. Furthermore, different types of technology use showed different influences on specific student outcomes. General technology uses were positively associated with student technology proficiency, while subject-specific technology uses were negatively associated with student technology proficiency. Social-communication technology uses were significantly positively associated with developmental outcomes such as self-esteem and positive attitude towards school. Entertainment/exploration technology use showed significant positive association with student learning habits. None of these technology uses had significant influence on student academic outcome.

Chen, Rong-Ji (2010) studied on Investigating Models for Preservice Teachers' Use of Technology to Support Student-Centered Learning. The study addressed two limitations of previous research on factors related to teachers' integration of technology in their teaching. It attempted to test a structural equation model (SEM) of the relationships among a set of variables influencing pre-service teachers' use of technology specifically to support student-centered learning. A review of literature led to a path model that provided the design and analysis for the study, which involved 206 -preservice teachers in the United States. The results show that the proposed model had a moderate fit to the observed data, and a more parsimonious model was found to have a better fit. In addition, pre-service teachers' self-efficacy of teaching with technology had the strongest influence on technology use, which was mediated by their perceived value of teaching and learning with technology. School's contextual factors had moderate influence on technology use. Moreover, the effect of pre-service teachers' training on student-centered technology use was mediated by both perceived value and self-efficacy of technology. The implications for teacher preparation include close collaboration between teacher education program and field experience, focusing on specific technology uses.

Eisenberg, Mike; Johnson, Doug; Berkowitz, Bob (2010) studied on Information, Communications, and Technology (ICT) Skills Curriculum Based on the Big6 Skills Approach to Information Problem-Solving. There is clear and widespread agreement among the public and educators that all students need to be proficient technology users. Technology literacy is among the attributes that appear in nearly every set of "21st Century Skills." However, while districts spend a great deal of money on technology, there seems to be only a vague notion of what technology literacy really means. Defining and describing technology skills is only a first step to assure all children become proficient information and technology users. Other critical elements will include a teacher-supported scope and sequence of skills, well designed projects, and effective assessments. Equally essential is fruitful collaboration among classroom teachers, teacher librarians, and technology teachers in order to present students with a unified and integrated approach to ensure that all children master the skills they will need to thrive in an information-rich future. This article presents the "Information, Communications, and Technology (ICT) Skills for Information Problem Solving" curriculum which defines technology capabilities and identifies associated skills based on the Big6 Skills Approach. The Curriculum describes levels of technology proficiency, and in so doing, promotes the skills and concepts basic to information and technology. In an information society, it is essential that students are technologically productive and able to solve information problems effectively and efficiently. This curriculum requires more than teaching computer skills, technology hardware, and software programs in an isolated approach. An effective technology curriculum must be integrated across content areas and grade levels to improve the learning process. Technology is successfully integrated when it seamlessly supports curricular goals. Students learn and refine their technology skills when they work on projects that require them to solve problems and make decisions.

Savage, Robert S.; Erten, Ozlem; Abrami, Philip; Hipps, Geoffrey; Comaskey, Erin; van Lierop, Dea (2010) studied on ABRACADABRA in the Hands of Teachers: The Effectiveness of a Web-Based Literacy Intervention in Grade 1 Language Arts Programs . Each teacher chose to use the program in qualitatively distinct ways that corresponded to the first three stages of Sandholtz, Ring staff, and Dwyer's (1997) technology integration model, namely: "Entry," "Adoption" and "Adaptation." Growth in literacy between pre- and post-test revealed significant differences associated with technology integration style across all measures of literacy and related language skills. The largest and most-widespread effects were evident for the "Adaptation" group that linked technology content to wider learning themes in the classroom. In terms of overall growth in standardized literacy scores across all six such measures used, Adaptation proved to be 60% more effective than Adoption. Results suggest that explorations of exactly how teachers use technology have important implications for practice as well as for the interpretation of field-based studies of the effectiveness of educational technology.

Jun, Han; Zhuzhu, Wang (2010) studied on Capability Building in Educational Technology for Teachers in China. This paper gives a brief introduction to the project called Education Technology Capacity Building Plan for All Primary and Secondary

Teachers now being implemented in China. Because information and communication technology skills training cannot match the demand of teachers' professional development, the Chinese Ministry of Education established the education technology standard for teachers and launched the project. This paper introduced the features of standard training and testing, and discusses the output and influence of the project.

McGarr, Oliver (2010) studied on Education for Sustainable Development in Technology Education in Irish Schools: A Curriculum Analysis. This paper explores the integration of Education for Sustainable Development (ESD) in technology education and the extent to which it is currently addressed in curriculum documents and state examinations in technology education at post-primary level in Ireland. This analysis is conducted amidst the backdrop of considerable change in technology education at post-primary level. The analysis of the provision of technology education found, that among the range of technology related subjects offered, the study of Technology and Society is only addressed in one in a comprehensive manner. The paper discusses the implications of this limited integration, examines the factors inhibiting greater integration of ESD and outlines opportunities for future development.

Waring, Scott M. (2010) studied on The Impact of a Technology Coordinator's Belief System upon Using Technology to Create a Community's History. As it has been shown that teachers of social studies content are less likely than teachers of other content areas to utilize technology in their classroom, this study focuses on one instructional technology coordinators' beliefs towards technology, instruction, and students and how these beliefs impacted how technology was utilized during a technology-enriched community history project with a group of fourth-grade students. It was determined that the instructional technology coordinators' beliefs included the following: (a) technology should serve as a tool and should be seamlessly integrated into the curriculum; (b) the teacher should construct meaningful experiences that allow students to become engaged in the learning process; however, before guiding student discovery, the teacher needs to explicitly teach basic technological skills; (c) and all students are able to learn and are capable of engaging in independent problem solving and critical thinking at some level. Her beliefs manifested themselves daily, particularly in the way that she approached instruction and integrated technology seamlessly into the curriculum. Through this study, it was found that the technology coordinator's beliefs toward technology, instruction, and her students directly impacted how technology was used in her classroom.

Jun, Han; Zhuzhu, Wang (2010) studied on Capability Building in Educational Technology for Teachers in China. This paper gives a brief introduction to the project called Education Technology Capacity Building Plan for All Primary and Secondary Teachers now being implemented in China. Because information and communication technology skills training cannot match the demand of teachers' professional development, the Chinese Ministry of Education established the education technology standard for teachers and launched the project. This paper introduced the features of standard training and testing, and discusses the output and influence of the project.

Ruzic-Dimitrijevic, Ljiljana; Dimitrijevic, Maja (2010) studied on Challenges IT Instructors Face in the Self-Education Process. We find that the earlier the instructors graduated, the smaller is the chance they studied the technologies similar to the ones they teach. We found that none of the surveyed instructors who graduated before 1979 teach a technology they studied. The analysis of the survey also supports the second hypothesis. The results show that 70% of the IT instructors have to change the course syllabus every 2-3 years due to the technology changes. We also found that the majority of the instructors primarily use textbooks and online tutorials to self teach new technologies, which support the third hypothesis. By comparison, they take courses given by others and work on real life projects far less often. In contrast, most instructors agree that taking courses and working on projects would greatly help them in their self-education. Most instructors (16 out of 20) assert that the lack of time stops them from doing so, which according to the survey is found to be one of the major challenges they face in the process of self-education, supporting the fourth hypothesis. Considering the results of our research, as well as our own experience, we have identified a list of activities that make the process of self-education more efficient and/or effective for IT instructors. These activities include taking on-line tutorials, creating software programs using the environment/ language/tools covered in the courses, working on real life projects, taking organized courses, attending IT/CS conferences, seminars, and workshops, collecting experience from industry people, and using the help of advanced students. However, in order to create the time for IT instructors to apply the self-learning methods and stay on top of the new technologies, we conclude that it may be necessary that the university policy include the time for self-learning as a significant part of IT instructors' everyday duties, i.e., as a part of their "job description".

Larson, Lotta; Kuhn, Cyndi Danner; Collins, Royce Ann; Balthazor, Gerri; Ribble, Mike; Miller, Teresa Northern (2009) studied on Technology Instruction: Fixing the Disconnect. High school students spend much of their educational journeys immersed in "old" literacy's of paper, pencil, and print books. But outside of the classroom, they are exposed to information and communication technologies—such as blogs, wikis, Internet browsers, multimedia, social networking sites, and a wide range of software—each of which demand new literacy's. This disconnect is a serious problem for schools because it reflects a decline in school's relevancy to students' futures, and the gap between how schools teach and how students learn will only grow over time.

The first step in updating a school's technology and instruction is to revisit and revise current vision statements by facilitating conversations with all stakeholders about expectations for student skills upon graduation. Vision setting must include the new literacy's. Teachers and education leaders must model expectations and support visionary teaching and learning through technology. To make that happen, they need instructional technology specialists who not only have a strong knowledge of hardware, networks, and equipment maintenance but also understand the art of teaching and how to enhance and enrich the daily curriculum by integrating technology. To do this, instructional technology staff members and those creating the curriculum must engage in ongoing dialogue to ensure that computer language is translated into the language of teaching and is directly related to what teachers want to do in their classrooms. For schools to successfully integrate technology, leaders must encourage and support strong relationships between teachers and technology support staff members. Schools must also provide easy access to technology in classrooms so that teachers can effectively integrate technology into the curriculum. Limited resources and complicated check-out procedures often contribute to lack of use. In addition, frustrations over blocked sites or limited access to online resources prevent teachers from integrating technology. Leaders, teachers, and technology staff members need ongoing communication with one another to share needs, frustrations, and solutions. Schools must move ahead quickly. It may be understandable for teachers and leaders to be a bit behind in the use of technology, but it is no longer adequate or appropriate to hold students back. Students today will be leaders in a global society, and technology can connect them to that world in ways that were unimaginable 10 years ago. School leaders need to join students in their world—which includes all of the new literacy's—so that everyone can function and contribute to the future.

Objectives

1. To study the level of teachers attitude towards using new technology in teaching
2. To find out whether there is any significant relationship between teachers attitude towards the use of new technology and their interest in teaching.

Methodology

The methodology adopted for the study is explained in detail. The sampling technique, size of the sample, variables of the study, description of the tool used and administration of tool are elaborated.

Sample

The study was conducted on 100 school teachers, Coimbatore district, Tamil Nadu.

Data Collection

Primary data, required for the present research work were collected by conducting direct interviews using questionnaire. All the respondents were given sufficient information about the study. These respondents were provided with the same questionnaires. They were also informed that they have to answer in the same fashion.

Analysis and Interpretation

Gender and attitude towards the use of new technology

Null Hypothesis No. 1.

There is no significant difference between male and female teachers attitude towards the use of new technology.

Table 1 : The Significance of the difference ('t' value) between mean scores of male and female teacher's attitude towards the use of new technology

Gender	N	Mean	SD	't' value	Level of Significance (0.05)
Male	50	100.30	11.81	4.89	Significant
Female	50	107.30	12.57		

It is evident from the table the calculated 't' value is 4.89 is significant at 0.05 level. Hence, the framed null hypothesis is rejected and research hypothesis is accepted. It is inferred that there is significant difference found between male and female teachers attitude towards the use of new technology.

Qualification and attitude towards the use of new technology

Null Hypothesis No. 2

There is no significant difference between undergraduate and post graduate teachers with respect to their attitude towards the use of new technology.

Table 2 : The significance of the difference ('t' value) between undergraduate and post graduate teachers with respect to their attitude towards the use of new technology.

Qualification	N	Mean	SD	't' value	Level of Significance (0.05)
Under graduate	35	103.64	11.44	0.28	Not Significant
Post graduate	65	103.23	13.53		

It is evident from the table the calculated 't' value is 0.28 which is not significant at 0.05 level. Hence, the framed null hypothesis is accepted. It shows that there is no significant difference between undergraduate and post graduate teachers with respect to their attitude towards the use of new technology.

Locality of the School and attitude towards the use of new technology

Null Hypothesis No. 3

There is no significant difference between rural and urban school teachers attitude towards the use of new technology.

Table 3 : The Significance of the difference ('t' value) between rural and urban school teachers attitude towards the use of new technology

Locality of the school	N	Mean	SD	't' value	Level of Significance (0.05)
Rural	65	103.42	11.23	0.06	Not Significant
Urban	35	103.33	14.15		

It is evident from the table the calculated 't' value is 0.06 which is not significant at 0.05 level. Hence, the framed null hypothesis is accepted. It shows that there is no significant difference between rural and urban school teachers attitude towards the use of new technology.

Type of School and attitude towards the use of new technology

Null Hypothesis No. 4

There is no significant difference between private and government school teachers attitude towards the use of new technology.

Table 4 : The Significance of the difference ('t' value) between private and government school teachers attitude towards the use of new technology

Type of school	N	Mean	SD	't' value	Level of Significance (0.05)
Private	65	104.79	11.54	1.26	Not Significant
Government	35	102.78	13.01		

It is evident from the table the calculated 't' value is 1.26 which is not significant at 0.05 level. Hence, the framed null hypothesis is accepted. It shows that there is no significant difference between private and government school teachers attitude towards the use of new technology.

Level of teaching and attitude towards the use of new technology

Null Hypothesis No. 5

There is no significant difference between secondary and higher secondary school teachers attitude towards the use of new technology.

Table 5 : The Significance of the difference ('t' test) between secondary and higher secondary school teachers attitude towards the use of new technology

Level of teaching	N	Mean	SD	't' value	Level of Significance (0.05)
Secondary School	60	102.12	12.12	1.85	Not Significant
Higher secondary School	40	104.82	13.03		

It is evident from the table the calculated 't' value is 1.85 which is not significant at 0.05 level. Hence, the framed null hypothesis is accepted. It is inferred that there is no significant difference between secondary and higher secondary school teachers attitude towards the use of new technology.

Teaching Experience and attitude towards the use of new technology

Null Hypothesis No. 6

There is no significant difference among teachers who have different years of teaching experience with respect to their attitude towards the use of new technology.

Table 6 : The Significance of the difference ('F' test) among school teachers with respect to their attitude towards the use of new technology

Teaching Experience	Sum of Squares	Mean Squares	df	'F' Value	Level of Significance (0.05)
Between Groups	2281.690	1140.845	2	7.48	Significant
Within Groups	45273.227	152.435	97		
Total	47554.917	-	99		

It is evident from the table the calculated 'F' value is 7.48 which is significant at 0.05 level. Hence, the framed null hypothesis is rejected and research hypothesis is accepted. It is inferred that there is significant difference among teachers who have different years of teaching experience with respect to their attitude towards the use of new technology.

Table 7 : The Significance of the difference ('t' test) between teachers who have different years of teaching experience with respect to their attitude towards the use of new technology

Teaching experience	N	Mean	SD	't' value	Level of Significance (0.05)
Below 10 years	49	109.33	11.05	3.06	Significant
10-20 years	20	103.03	12.80		
Above 20 years	31	101.67	12.47	4.16	Significant
Below 10 years	49	109.33	11.05		
10-20 years	20	103.03	12.80	0.81	Not Significant
Above 20 years	31	101.67	12.47		

From table, it is revealed that there is significant difference between teachers who have below 10 years of teaching experience and 10-20 years of teaching experience and teachers who have above 20 years of teaching experience and below 10 years of teaching experience. Whereas no significant difference is found between teachers who have above 20 years of teaching experience and 10-20 years of teaching experience.

Correlation Analysis

Correlation Analysis between teachers attitude towards the use of new technology and interest in teaching

One of the important objectives of the present investigation is to study the significant relationship between teacher's attitude towards the use of new technology and interest in teaching. For this purpose, the investigator applied the co-efficient of correlation ('r'). The computed values are given in the table. The investigator also framed a null hypothesis for testing the relationship between teacher's attitude towards the use of new technology and interest in teaching.

Null hypothesis No. 8

There is no significant relationship between teacher's attitude towards the use of new technology and interest in teaching.

Table 8 : Co-efficient of Correlation between teacher's attitude towards the use of new technology and interest in teaching

Correlation	N	'r' value	Level of Significance at 0.05 level
Teacher's attitude towards the use of new technology and interest in teaching	100	0.56	Significant

It is evident from the table the computed correlation coefficient 'r' for entire sample is 0.56, which is significant at 0.05 level. Hence, the framed null hypothesis is rejected. It is inferred that there is significant relationship found between teacher's attitude towards the use of new technology and their interest in teaching.

Suggestions

The present study gives a clear-cut view about the present position of teachers attitude towards the use of new technology and their interest in teaching. Based on the important findings stated earlier the following recommendations are suggested.

1. Teachers must be provided with adequate opportunities to enhance their knowledge in new technologies and equipments. The government should provide more effective environment through schools for them to improve their skills in application of new technologies in teaching.
2. Periodical in-service training programmes should be organized to keep their interest and quest in teaching.

3. The finding of the present study reveals that the teachers have neutral attitude towards the use of new technology in teaching and low interest in teaching. This indicates that the Heads of the institutions must look into the varied problems that influence the interest of teachers and find amicable solutions to their difficulties.
4. More activities should be planned in the curriculum to bring forth different modes of creative expressions which will provide competition and generate interest of teachers in teaching.
5. Sincere work and involved performances of teachers must be recognized and honoured by the authorities. And application of innovative methods and technologies in instruction must be encouraged.
6. In addition with the above recommendation the government and all the other concerned authorities should realize the problems of experienced teachers and provide conductive environment of growth and mutual help of teachers should be ensured.

Conclusion

The present study is conducted on teachers attitude towards the use of new technologies in teaching and their interest in teaching. The findings of the present study revealed that the teachers have neutral attitude towards the use of new technology and low interest in teaching. Therefore, the authorities and government should find suitable measures to improve the interest of teachers in teaching and the application of innovative technologies in Teaching Learning Process.

References

1. Larson, Lotta; Kuhn, Cyndi Danner; Collins, Royce

Ann; Balthazor, Gerri; Ribble, Mike; Miller, Teresa Northern (2009) Technology Instruction: Fixing the Disconnect. Principal Leadership, v10 n4 p54-58.

2. Chen, Rong-Ji (2010) Investigating Models for Preservice Teachers' Use of Technology to Support Student-Centered Learning. Computers & Education, v55 n1 p32-42.
3. Eisenberg, Mike; Johnson, Doug; Berkowitz, Bob (2010) Information, Communications, and Technology (ICT) Skills Curriculum Based on the Big6 Skills Approach to Information Problem-Solving. Library Media Connection, v28 n6 p24-27.
4. Jun, Han; Zhuzhu, Wang(2010) Capability Building in Educational Technology for Teachers in China British Journal of Educational Technology, v41 n4 p607-611.
5. Lei, Jing (2010) Quantity versus Quality: A New Approach to Examine the Relationship between Technology Use and Student Outcomes. 2010.
6. Lesisko, Lee J.; Wright, Robert J.; O'Hern, Brenda (2010) Technology Integration: A Best Practice Perspective. Online Submission, Paper presented at the Annual Meeting of the Eastern Educational Research Association (Savannah, GA, Feb 10-13, 2010).
7. McGarr, Oliver (2010) Education for Sustainable Development in Technology Education in Irish Schools: A Curriculum Analysis. International Journal of Technology and Design Education, v20 n3 p317-332.
8. Ruzic-Dimitrijevic, Ljiljana; Dimitrijevic, Maja (2010) Challenges IT Instructors Face in the Self-Education Process. Journal of Information Technology Education, v9 pIIP-35-IIP-48.

9. Savage, Robert S.; Erten, Ozlem; Abrami, Philip; Hipps, Geoffrey; Comaskey, Erin; van Lierop, Dea (2010) ABRACADABRA in the Hands of Teachers: The Effectiveness of a Web-Based Literacy Intervention in Grade 1 Language Arts Programs . Computers & Education, v55 n2 p911-922.

10. Shapley, Kelly; Sheehan, Daniel; Maloney, Catherine; Caranikas-Walker, Fanny (2010) Effects of Technology Immersion on Teachers' Growth in Technology Competency, Ideology, and Practices. Journal of Educational Computing Research, v42 n1 p1-33.

11. Waring, Scott M. (2010) The Impact of a Technology Coordinator's Belief System upon Using Technology to Create a Community's History. Computers in the Schools, v27 n2 p76-98.

13

An Assessment of Edu Digital Skills

Introduction

Teacher is an ideal personality whose knowledge and skill play a major role in the development of the nation to the global standard education in general and tapping the potentialities of students to the maximum extent in particular. Teachers are expected to learn forever to withstand the innovations in teaching and updating the knowledge and widen the clarity of the conceptual framework of the subject of specialization too. Unless and until the teachers prepared to meet the requirements and challenges, the dream and purpose of education will not be fulfilled. Nowadays the system of education has assumed the character which involves more students' participation and student centric which is highly enabled through the application of various educational technologies. Edu - digital skills is considered prerequisite for all teachers teaching for nursery to doctorate scholars. 21st century school curriculum has been enriched to meet the demands of world requirements of quality. Communication, collaboration, critical thinking, problem solving, creativity, invention, information and technology literacy and self direction will facilitate the achievement of aims and objectives of education. Teachers of 21st century are expected to equip themselves with modern technology application in teaching and learning process. A paradigm shift has happened to meet the demands of gen y and z learners which require innovative, explorative and interesting approach in teaching and learning. The curriculum will need withstand the futuristic vision for the global scenario. At this juncture the teachers of today should be enthusiastic to update their knowledge and skills forever in order to keep young to the youngest generation whom they meet and it may also be emphasized greatly as the professional ethics. This study has been attempted to assess the knowledge and skills of teachers in the field of information and communication technology which a teacher necessarily possess in the digital world.

Educational Digital Skills

It is mentioned that in order to thrive in a digital economy, students will need digital age proficiencies. It is important for the educational system to make parallel changes in order to fulfill its mission in society, namely the preparation of students for the world beyond the classroom. Therefore, the educational system must understand and embrace the following 21st century skills within the context of rigorous academic standards.

The 21st Century Literacy Summit (2002) contends that “the explosive growth of technology in every aspect of society offers us a unique opportunity to engage our citizens in economic and civic life” The report further states that to take advantage of this opportunity, we must continually acquire and develop new knowledge and skills. Summit participants noted “Information and communication technologies are raising the bar on the competencies needed to succeed in the 21st century, and they are compelling us to revisit many of our assumptions and beliefs”

The sheer magnitude of human knowledge, world to technology necessitates a shift in our children's education - from plateaus of knowing to continuous cycles of learning. Therefore, policymakers and educators alike must define 21st century skills, highlighting the relationship of those skills to conventional academic standards. As they do so, they must also recognize the need for multiple assessments to measure these skills within the context of academic standards, evaluating their application to today's technological and global society.

Technological Literacy

Demonstrate a sound conceptual understanding of the nature of technology systems and view themselves as proficient users of these systems. Understand and model positive, ethical use of technology in both social and personal contexts. Use a variety of technology tools in effective ways to increase creative productivity. Use communication tools to reach out to the world beyond the classroom and communicate ideas in powerful ways. Use technology effectively to access, evaluate, process and synthesize information from a variety of sources. Use technology to identify and solve complex problems in real-world contexts have been considered as Technological Literacy

Information Literacy

Before Accessing Information one should determine what is known and what is needed for problem solving, identify different sources of information, including text, people, video, audio, and databases and prioritize sources based on credibility and relevance. When Accessing Information one need identify and retrieve relevant information from sources and use technology to enhance searching. Revise information-gathering strategies that prove to be in effective when understands how information retrieved does or does not address original problem, evaluate information in terms of credibility and know what are the social, economic, political, legal, and ethical issues that may impact it to facilitate to use technology for evaluation. After Information is extracted, using retrieved information to accomplish a specific purpose, present information clearly and persuasively by using a range of technology tools and media and evaluate the processes and products of these activities have here been considered essential to assure one to be Literate in information.

Global Awareness

Global awareness is knowledge about the connectedness of the nations of the world historically, politically, economically, technologically, socially, linguistically, and ecologically and understand that these interconnections of positive benefits and negative consequences too. The ability to recognize, analyzes, and evaluates major trends in global relations and the interconnections of these trends with both their local and national communities. Participate in the global society by staying current with international news and by participating in the democratic process.

Objectives of the Study

To find the level of Edu-digital skill among school teachers and find whether there is significant different exist among them in relation to their personal variables such as sex, Age, Educational Qualification, Area of Residence, Management of the Institution, Subject of Specialization and the Location of the School.

Research Question

What is the level of educational digital Skills of School Teachers? Is there any Significant Difference Exists among them with respect to their Personal Variables?

Research Methodology

A Normative Descriptive Method of study has been attempted to assess the level of Educational Digital Skills among the School Teachers in Namakkal District

Population, Sample and Sampling Technique of the Study

All teachers who teach in school education are the population of the study and the sample of the study has been chosen from teachers work in Namakkal district only and the sample was taken by stratified random sampling technique which consists of 250.

Tools and Technique of Data Collection

A tool consisted of 24 items related to some basic skills necessary for adopting computer enabled teaching technology, using internet connection which will benefit students to gain knowledge, understand the concept better, improve the critical thinking, problem solving ability, creativity and to enhance their communication skill and appropriate application of the knowledge gained for the betterment of himself and to the society. The scope of this study extent all teachers who teach in the classroom from kindergarten to plus two levels. The questionnaire has dimensions of using the computer for retrieving useful information via internet, knowledge about various search engines, and preparation of effective PowerPoint materials, video clippings, software package application, audio recording, connecting to virtual classroom and the facilities to publish the students works in internet. Knowledge and the application of MS word, Excel format, mobile for teaching and learning purpose and the ability to set ready LCD, mike and arrange show in the smart classroom and the application of social media in education have also been taken for assessing.

Scoring Procedure & Statistical Tools Used

The Questionnaire used in the study has five point scale of the level of skill of the respondents in relation to their digital skill hence it has five options of known very well, known, moderately known, known little and Unknown which scored as 5, 4,3,2 and 1 respectively.

SPSS package has been used to analyze the data and the percentage analysis and the differential analysis have been used to describe and infer the details pertaining to the research question formulated for the study.

Table -1 : An Analysis of Edu Digital Skills among Teachers in Namakkal District

Items	Very well Known		Well Known		Moderately Known		Known Little		Unknown		Total
	F	%	F	%	F	%	F	%	F	%	
Information Retrieval	41	16.4	59	23.6	62	24.8	75	30	13	5.2	250
Power point preparation	52	20.8	67	26.8	53	21.2	60	24	18	7.2	250
Efficient use of Windows operating system	35	14	48	19.2	75	30	81	32.4	11	4.4	250
Connecting to the Online Teaching of World Classroom	15	6	20	8	39	15.6	116	46.4	60	24	250
Skill in make it work well of LCD mike screen view	15	6	26	10.4	77	30.8	114	45.6	18	7.2	250

Knowledge about E learning material preparation	21	8.4	15	6	27	10.8	129	51.6	58	23.2	250
Account in social networking sites like Face-book, twitter	22	8.8	36	14.4	74	29.6	12	4.8	106	42.4	250
Using of videos and computer games in teaching	19	7.6	29	11.6	55	22	85	34	62	24.8	250
Application of Virtual classrooms and chat rooms in teaching and learning	13	5.2	18	7.2	17	6.8	56	22.4	146	58.4	250
Application of documentary film in deliverance of the instructional objectives	51	20.4	60	24	41	16.4	31	12.4	67	26.8	250
Using of web-Camera in virtual interaction	16	6.4	41	16.4	27	10.8	71	28.4	95	38	250
Application of white Board in teaching	25	10	16	6.4	19	7.6	43	17.2	147	58.8	250
Safety and security issues in using webmail	17	6.8	39	15.6	90	36	70	28	44	17.6	250

Security Challenges in instant messaging	15	6	35	14	78	31.2	98	39.2	24	9.6	250
Application of iPod and tables in teaching	11	4.4	23	9.2	67	26.8	80	32	69	27.6	250
Application of Video conferencing for teaching and learning	32	12.8	24	9.6	71	28.4	90	36	33	13.2	250
Application of YouTube	49	19.6	86	34.4	55	22	62	24.8	38	15.2	250
Application of Flicker & Picasa	19	7.6	25	10	62	24.8	104	41.6	40	16	250
Application of mobile phone for transferring data of video	21	8.4	27	10.8	80	32	90	36	32	12.8	250
Application of mobile phone for transferring data of voice	22	8.8	33	13.2	76	30.4	81	32.4	38	15.2	250
Application of mobile phone for transferring data of text	187	74.8	46	18.4	3	1.2	9	3.6	5	2	250
Assessment of students performance through online	25	10	52	20.8	58	23.2	105	42	10	4	250

Application of learning Management System - LMS	11	4.4	21	8.4	37	14.8	57	22.8	15	6	250
Application of Video-recording	17	6.8	26	10.4	51	20.4	78	31.2	78	31.2	250

Majority of teachers have necessary in Skill and knowledge in the application of MS office, Mobile technology in teaching and learning, information retrieval system from online resource centre but the majority teachers have moderate and least knowledge about e-content preparation, application of social media, and security issues in web mails, various learning management system and efficient use of ICT in teaching

Table-2 : Significance of Difference in Edu-Digital Skill of Teachers

Demographic Variables	**P Value**	**Level of Sig.**
Sex	0.153	NS
Area of Residence	0.104	NS
Location of the School	0.214	NS
Teaching Experience	0.098	NS
Educational Qualification	0.521	NS
Management of the School	0.021*	S
Subject of Specialization	0.001**	S

There is no significant difference exist among the respondents in their Educational digital skill in relation to their personal variables of Sex, Area of Residence, Location of the School, Teaching Experience and their educational qualification. But the statistical report of analysis shows that there is significant difference exist among the sample in relation to their management of the school and their subject of specialization.

Educational Implications

a) Teacher Education curriculum should emphasize the ICT enabled education in B.Ed program

b) Workshops need to be conducted for B.Ed program in the practical application of ICT and training program can be organized for E- content preparation

c) Orientation and Refresher courses for the teachers in schools should be conducted frequently to enable teachers to facilitate them in the efficient use of ICT in teaching and learning environment

d) Collaborative Approach should be made in integrating ICT in education

Conclusion

Teachers are the forerunner of all developments and growth of the nation and the world; they play a significant role in bringing desirable outcome in the world with their adaptability and their ever learning behavior of updating knowledge and skills in any field. No technology can replace the teacher in any period of time but the teacher needs possess skills in the application of technology which facilitate desirable educational outcome in the field of education.

References

1. Felix.A & Jahitha Begum (2011) "An Awareness of E-resources related to ICT and Education among M.Ed Students and M.Phil Scholars" ICT in teaching and learning, APH Publishing Corporation, New Delhi, p.169

2. Nagarajan .K (2009) "Educational Innovations and Management" Ram Publishers, Chennai. Pp.135-185.

3. Natchimuthu.K (2012), "Need of E-Content Development in Education Today" APH Publication Corporation, New Delhi. P.76.

4. Rangarajan. P & Senthilnathan.S (2012) "Teacher Educators Attitude towards E Learning" Edutracks, Vol.No.12 No.1 pp. 21-32.

5. www.educatorstechnology.com/2012/06/33-digital-skills-every-21st-century.htm

6. http://www.educatorstechnology.com/2013/07/the-8-digital-skills-students-need-for.html

14

Learning Without Limit-kinds of Learning

Introduction

"'Creating Learning without Limits' takes on one of the most important issues in education today. In the last decade schools in have taken a path towards putting all children into boxes, attaching a level to their heads and deciding what they are capable of achieving. The possibility of a different educational path, one in which all students are encouraged to achieve the greatest they can. Importantly the book also documents ways in which courageous teachers can do this - promoting fair and engaging learning environments for all students. This is a must-read for educators, policy makers and parents alike.""This will undoubtedly turn out to be amongst the most important educational books of the decade. Our capacity to respond, both individually and collectively, to its key insights and messages will profoundly affect not just the quality of our schools, but of our society for years to come. It reminds us why people come into education - to make a difference for children. To make a deep difference we have to organize education differently. It describes a school that vibrates with learning in an atmosphere of deep humanity and care. Its practices are light years away from the measuring, labeling, targeting, and testing structures that have become our recent national norm. The school as a whole community transforms people."

"The self-confidence that comes from a profound faith in the capacity of every child to be a passionate and engaged learner. This in the face of powerful and societal dominant messages that explicitly or more insidiously tell a different and more deterministic tale: that children (and schools) are fit and proper subjects for classification, measurement and management. And there's more - the careful scholarship on which this story is based prevents this book from being merely a description of what happens when a unique constellation of propitious circumstances meets a charismatic leader: this 'other way' is open to all who will take it - but it will demand the laying of solid and value-rich foundations, the exercising of autonomy for staff and pupils, the rethinking of relationships, a focus on learning (letting performance come as a secondary gift), and the taking of collective action. It's become a cliché to say of a book that it 'should be read by every teacher (or parent, or whoever ...).' This one, and its predecessor 'Learning withoutLimits"meritsthatinjunction."

Many students would likely cite a desire to learn. Students assume that, because they have read their text and memorized facts, they have learned something. Definition of 'learn' in a dictionary step, Step1. To acquire knowledge of a subject or skill through education or experience, Step2. To gain information about somebody or something. Step3. To memorize something. This definition is not particularly insightful, although it reminds us that the word can be used to describe the acquisition of both knowledge and skill, and that acquisition can be by a variety of means. Including education experience, or memorization.

The Current Situation

The American education system is considered among the best in the world. More than 50% of our nation's high school graduates continue on to college and each year our universities and colleges enroll thousands of students from other countries. Despite these statistics, several recent studies have shown that many college seniors have neither good general knowledge nor the necessary skills for reasoning in today's society. At the end of the course, the test scores of those students who had completed the economics course were only 20% better than those who had not taken the course, and this difference dropped to less than 10% seven years after completion of the course. The results and many others, strongly suggest that our current instructional practices are not working and that many students are not learning, or retaining what they do learn.

Need for New Kinds of Learning

There have been calls for new kinds of learning from many different parts of society. College teachers have expressed frustration about attendance in class, uncompleted reading assignments, and students focus on grades rather than learning. Student surveys indicate that courses are not interesting, that students fail to recognize the value of what they are learning, and that many faculty rely too heavily on lectures for transmitting information. The 1996 National Science Foundation report on shaping the future urges faculty to promote new kinds of learning that include developing skills in communication, teamwork, and lifelong learning. Gardiner(1994) compiled a list of critical competencies for citizens and workers from leaders in business, industry and government.

1. Personal responsibility.
2. Ability to act in principled, ethical fashion
3. Skill in oral and written communication

4. Interpersonal and team skills
5. Skills in critical thinking and problem-solving
6. Respect for people different from oneself,
7. Ability to change
8. Ability and desire for lifelong learning.

Society and individual learners now have different needs, both in terms of what people need to learn and how they can and should learn. It is a great nuisance that knowledge can be acquired only by hard work-Somerset Maugham.

Different kinds of thinking and learning

In cognitive theory and education have used Bloom's (1956) taxonomic of learning. Bloom and colleagues identified three learning domains. The cognitive domains involve thinking of all sorts. The affective domain includes feelings, emotions, attitude, values and motivations.

The psychomotor domain of learning includes physical movement, coordination, motor, and sensory-skills. When a learning experience has a profound effect on a student, it can result in a greater sense of caring for the subject, for them, other or learning in general. Greater caring can lead to new interests, energy for learning, or a change in values. 'To learn how to learn' this includes learning how to diagnose one's own need for learning and how to be a self-learner. Then type of learning enables students to continue learning with greater effectiveness and is a particularly important skill with the recent explosion of knowledge and technology.

Learning and the Brain

Many people both young and old enjoy solving problems. These observation suggest that the human brain has a fundamental need to solve problems and understand its surroundings. New understanding of the working of the brain.

1. Learning changes the physical structure of the brain.
2. Learning organized and reorganizes the brain.
3. Different parts of the brain may be ready to learn at different stages of development.

Experience equate to learning, the brain is a dynamic organ. Learning in individual and social contexts actually results in new pattern of organization and improved functioning of the brain.

Critical Thinking

"A tool for everyone" Critical thinking is so central to sound reasoning that it deserves special attention. The methods of critical thought arc by no means limited to thinking in science, but have also been applied in virtually all other disciplines. They involve both cognitive and affective components. Critical thinking is the intellectually disciplined process of actively and skillfully conceptualizing, applying, analyzing, synthesizing and evaluating information gathered from or generated by observation experience, reflection, reasoning or communication as a guide to belief and action. National Council for Excellence in Critical Thinking, Paul and Elder(2004)

Thinking About One's Own Thinking and Learning

Intentional thought about one's own thinking is generally regarded as an essential component of successful thinkers and learners monitor their understanding and progress during problem solving. I went to a bookstore and asked the sales-woman, "Where's the self-help section?" She said if she told me, it would defeat the purpose-George Carlin

Effective Learning and Learning Styles

Best learning occurs when students are engaged in active learning- when they are doing things instead of sitting passively and listening. In a recent review of the effectiveness of active learning, Prince(2004) found extensive, widespread support for active learning approaches, especially when activities were designed around important learning outcomes and promoted thoughtful engagement. Many instructors recognize that active learning results in significant improvements in student knowledge retention, conceptual understanding, engagement, and attitudes about learning.

A commonly used approach in active learning is cooperative learning. An enormous body of research confirms the effectiveness of cooperative learning. Compared with more traditional individualized and competitive models of learning, students who learn in cooperative groups exhibit markedly improved individual achievement.

Conclusion

There are many different ways of modeling the way of learning. No one model provides a complete description of learning, and no single learning style is superior to another. However, it is important to be aware of your own learning style preferences so that you can make the necessary adjustments to maximize your learning. Unfamiliar pedagogies example active learning, cooperative learning. These have largely been designed to teach to a wide variety of learning styles and to facilitate learning the content and skills encompassed within significant learning. Some of these new instructional approaches keep an open mind and try to understand the objectives of each pedagogical approach. If you have questions about classroom methods, ask your instructor. Most teachers are happy to discuss instructional practices with their students.

Bibliography of Learning:

1. AACU,2002, Greater Expectations: A New Vision for Learning as a Nation Goes to College: National panel Report, American Association of Colleges and Universities, Washington,DC62p.
2. Atkinson,R.L Atkinson R.C Smith, E.E and Bem D.J., 1993, Introduction to Psychology, Harcourt Brace Jovanovich, Fort Worth, TX, 11th edition
3. Cuesta College, 2004, Characteristics of a Successful Student: Cuesta College. Available at:
4. http://academic. Cuesta.edu/accasupp/as/201.HTM.
5. Johnson, D.W., Johnson, R.T., and Smith, K., 1991,Active Learning: Cooperation in the College Classroom Interaction Book Company,Edina,MN.
6. Krathwohl, D.R.Bloom, B.S, and Masia,B.B., 1964, Taxonomy of Educational objectives. The classification of Educational Goals, Handbook II: Affective Domain. David McKay Company,Inc
7. Teaching Goals Inventory,2004, Available form: http://www.uiowa.edu/-centeach/tgi/.
8. Williams,John,H., 1993, Clarifying grade expectations. The Teaching Professor, August/September.

15

Latest Technology For Teachers

Introduction

This paper discusses the Flipped Classroom: The Latest Technology for Teachers. All across the nation and beyond, teachers are experimenting with flipping the classroom. They are flipping instruction. The basic concept is quite simple. Homework gets done in the class work while class instruction occurs at home. With the flipped classroom concept, the teacher becomes less of a "sage on the stage" and more of a "guide on the side." This is done by having students watch pre-recorded lessons on screen or pod casts online at home. The next day, class lecture time is freed up to have the students put their newly acquired knowledge into practice.

Technology has changed the way of doing everything, and education is no exception. Flipping the classroom can be as simple or as elaborate as the teacher wants to make it. Low-tech teachers can flip classroom instruction with a simple-made video he or she makes, or choose one from shared files. High-tech teachers will explore software and technologies to enhance the flipped classroom learning experience. This enhancement can be in the way of shareware such as Edmodo or learnspace. These sites are like having facebook accounts private to you and your students. Teachers can post quizzes, due dates, etc. on line. Students can post and form groups for working on projects together. Files too large to share by email can be sent.

Videos can be viewed on computers, laptops, iPads Smartphones, etc. Students with no computer access (rare these days) can be given a spot in the classroom, computer lab or media center. This is also a good place for students who may need to review the material while in school.

The Flipped Class: What it is and what it is not

There has been a lot of interest in the flipped classroom.

The traditional definition of a flipped class is: Where videos take the place of direct instruction

1. This then allows students to get individual time in class to work with their teacher on key learning activities.
2. It is called the flipped class because what used to be class work (the "lecture" is done at home via teacher-created videos and what used to be homework (assigned problems) is now done in class.

But from our perspective, as successful flipped teachers, everyone believes it is so much more. People also realize there is a lot of mis-information about the Flipped Classroom and quite a bit of controversy about whether or not this is a viable instructional methodology. Thus the purpose of this article is to list out what one believes it is and what one believes it is not.

The Flipped Classroom is NOT

A synonym for online videos. When most people hear about the flipped class all they think about are the videos. It is the interaction and the meaningful learning activities that occur during the face-to-face time that is most important.

1. About replacing teachers with videos.
2. An online course.
3. Students working without structure.
4. Students spending the entire class staring at a computer screen.
5. Students working in isolation.

The Flipped Classroom IS

A means to INCREASE interaction and personalized contact time between students and teachers.

1. An environment where students take responsibility for their own learning.
2. A classroom where the teacher is not the "sage on the stage", but the "guide on the side".
3. A blending of direct instruction with constructivist learning.
4. A classroom where students who are absent due to illness or extra-curricular activities such as athletics or field-trips, don't get left behind.
5. A class where content is permanently archived for review or remediation.
6. A class where all students are engaged in their learning.
7. A place where all students can get a personalized education.

The flipped classroom seems to be the latest buzz in educational trends. Is this truly a new revolutionary approach or a revision of a technique used throughout the ages? To be clear, in simplest terms, flipping the classroom refers to swapping classroom lecture time for hands-on practice time. So the lecture is done for homework usually via a video or audio file and the classroom time is spent clarifying and applying new knowledge gained.

A survey of the latest literature indicates that flipping a classroom is not a new idea. It is the way that idea is applied that is gaining so much attention and in most cases, so much praise. Many say that reversing the content delivery and practice is a decades old practice. Consider literature classes where the student reads the novel outside of class. Class time is spent discussing themes and archetypes and rarely the plot of the story. Law schools also traditionally flip when students participate in Socratic seminars and must prepare ahead of time to effectively participate in the seminar and have knowledge to back up their statements (Berrett, 2012). So if it is not something new in education, why is it attracting headlines and discussions?

First a little history on the recent re-emergence of this time tested class technique. It seems that the confluence of enlightenment that led to the current use of the term "flipped classroom" originates in three or four different situations. While high school science teachers Jonathan Bergmann and Aaron Sams of Woodland Park, CO are most often credited with coining the phrase flipped classroom in 2007 (White, 2011), there are other schools and programs that essentially developed the same concept around the same time, albeit after.

Dr. Eric Mazur, a physicist at Harvard University, has been using the method for 21 years. With the addition of assistive technology to allow for student response and feedback during the peer instruction session, attendees saw how this process works to maximize time with the instructor and focus on higher order thinking skills rather than just taking notes and regurgitating facts.

Some of the characteristics of this latest iteration include engaging the students on a higher level and a smaller ratio of students to instructors while working within the economics of education. As Dr. Mazur said: "Once you engaged the students' minds, there's an eagerness to learn, to be right, to master" (Berrett, 2012). According to Bloom (1984), "an average student who receives one-on-one attention is enabled by constant feedback and corrective process, and can jump into the 98th percentile of the student population in academic achievement" (Houston and Lin, 2012). This was stated 24 years ago but most classes are still taught with teacher-centered lectures and only the persistent students seek out one-on-one assistance.

Lecture as a teaching technique is not going away. Economics dictate that class size will not decrease to lower the student-to-instructor ratio. Therefore, lecturing makes economic sense. Flipping and moving the lecture to the homework realm and saving application and one-on-one work for the classroom experience makes the lecture model more productive. Implementing a flipped classroom enables more focused teaching and learning to take place in the classroom.

Effectively flipping a classroom brings many benefits. Flipping uses technology to remove passive, one-way lecturing as the only means of teaching. Thus, the instructor and students can interact within the newly gained instructional time (Houston and Lin, 2012). The increase of teacher-student interaction during class time is what characterizes its success (White, 2012). The classroom time is used to solve problems and apply to other contexts (the application of higher order thinking skills).

Flipping the classroom also makes differentiating instruction based on students' needs easier because everyone does not necessarily need to do the same task in class (Liles, 2012). Simply looking at the perceived and real benefits of flipping as well as the amount of research recently done should be incentive to consider a flip as a great way to reach students and approach mastery of content.

Transformational Potential of Flipped Classrooms

In the flipped classroom, the teacher is available to guide students as they apply what they have learned online. One of the drawbacks of traditional homework is that students don't receive meaningful feedback on their work while they are doing it; they may have no opportunity to relearn concepts they struggled to master. With a teacher present to answer questions and watch over how students are doing, the feedback cycle has greater potential to bolster student learning.

The flipped classroom does not address all the limitations of the brick-and-mortar school. Although in the best flipped-classroom implementations, each student can move at her own pace and view lessons at home that meet her individual needs rather than those of the entire class, most flipped classrooms do not operate this way. As Salman Khan, the media's personification of the flipped-classroom, observes in The One World Schoolhouse, "Although it makes class time more interactive and lectures more independent, the 'flipped classroom' still has students moving together in age-based cohorts at roughly the same pace, with snapshot exams that are used more to label students than address their weaknesses" (see "To YouTube and Beyond," book reviews, Summer 2013).

This arrangement also doesn't tackle the root causes of the lack of motivation that persists among many low-achieving students.

Some in the media have suggested that the flipped-classroom approach may only work in upper-income, suburban schools. If low-income students lack access to computers at home or to reliable Internet access, flipping may be a nonstarter in some schools. If students can't benefit from online instruction at home, then they need to receive instruction in the classroom or risk falling behind. Some fear that in relying on parents to provide technology and support, the flipped-classroom model may exacerbate existing resource inequalities. Schools can make computer labs available during after school hours, however, and parental assistance is less critical when watching an online video than when solving homework problems.

What is perhaps most telling is that the "no-excuses" charter schools that serve large numbers of low-income students well—KIPP, Rocket ship, Alliance, and Summit among them—are not flipping their classrooms. Even as these schools adopt blended-learning models, the flipped classroom isn't among them. The models these schools are employing give students more support as they need it and actively guide students to more ownership over their learning. These models also do not rely on students having access to high-speed Internet-connected computers at home; online learning occurs during the school day.

Even if the flipped classroom does prove of some benefit to some low-income students, this change in structure alone is unlikely to produce the vast improvement in student learning our country needs.

But that doesn't mean the innovation is insignificant. The flipped classroom might still have an important indirect impact on the American education system, as one brand of digital learning. The optimal use of digital learning will vary in different contexts and communities. Some people will attend full-time virtual schools, with even the "classroom" experience occurring online; most will attend brick-and-mortar schools that employ some version of digital learning.

Unlike school vouchers for low-income students, charter schools in disadvantaged communities, or bonus pay for teachers in inner-city schools, digital learning is not designed for just one slice of the population. It's not a policy that parents might support in theory but, because it has no practical impact on them, won't spend political energy promoting or defending. Rather, if it works as well as its proponents hope, digital learning will gather political support from a wide swath of the American public. And it may well turn out that the flipped classroom is most effective in private schools or upper-income suburban schools. If that's how those students make the best use of digital learning, that's OK. As Khan says, "Blue jeans didn't become cool until Hollywood started wearing them." In the world of digital learning, the flipped classroom may just be one good brand.

The purpose of flipping the classroom is to shift from passive to active learning to focus on the higher order thinking skills such as analysis, synthesis and evaluation (Bloom). As explained in this short video, Flipping the Classroom: Simply Speaking (Penn State), students access key content individually (or in small groups) prior to class time and then meet face-to-face in the larger group to explore content through active learning and engagement strategies.

There are many permutations of what a flipped classroom will look like and depends on variables such as class size, resources, support and readiness to change. At UQ, several teachers across the faculties have already flipped their classrooms and their valuable experiences have been captured in the Studies section.

In the flipped classroom, the roles and expectations of students and teachers change where: students take more responsibility for their own learning and study core content either individually or in groups before class and then apply knowledge and skills to a range of activities using higher order thinking, teaching 'one-to-many' focuses more on facilitation and moderation than lecturing, though lecturing is still important. Significant learning opportunities can be gained through facilitating active learning, engaging students, guiding learning, correcting misunder-standings and providing timely feedback using a variety of pedagogical strategies, there is a greater focus on concept exploration, meaning making and demonstration or application of knowledge in the face-to-face setting (see Diagram 1 below).

Educational technologies (see Diagram 2) are an important feature of the flipped classroom as they can be used to:

1. capture key content for students to access at their own convenience and to suit their pace of learning (e.g. lecture material, readings, interactive multimedia),

2. present learning materials in a variety of formats to suit different learner styles (e.g. text, videos, audio, multimedia),

3. provide opportunities for discourse and interaction in and out of class (e.g. polling tools, discussion tools, content creation tools),

4. convey timely information, updates and reminders for students (e.g micro-blogging, announcement tools),

5. provide immediate and anonymous feedback for teachers and students (e.g. quizzes, polls) to signal revision points,

6. capture data about students to analyse their progress and identify 'at risk' students (e.g. analytics).

Sample Plan for Flipped Instruction

The objective is to understand and apply the scientific method. Students will identify dependent variable, independent variable, control group, hypothesis,

1. Build motivation and create a "hook" for anticipating learning with a PowerPoint presentation or text book reading. Include a short quiz either online or with pencil/ paper. Whatever your level of technology is at this point. Don't worry; there is no need to be a techie to do this. Give points for completing the presentation.

2. Create or import a lesson/lecture on the basics of the scientific method. It's a good beginning. It is best if you make these videos yourself, but it's OK to use other videos Check for understanding with a quiz, online or paper/ pencil.
3. Review with questioning at the beginning or class
4. Assign directions for a project:
5. Purpose: Create a lab to demonstrate the scientific method using a simple paper airplane.
6. Make a hypothesis: Decide on a plan and make a prediction based on the procedure you have developed to use the paper airplane.
7. Develop a plan that demonstrates the scientific method. Try to create a table and a graph to record collected data. Have students do 10 trials.
8. Have students write two paragraphs analyzing collected data.

Advantages of Flipped Instruction

Flipped instruction can be used in almost any classroom to a degree. Just remember the basic concept. Classroom instruction becomes homework and homework becomes classroom work. This frees up much time for active learning in the classroom. Teachers can plan hands-on activities for students that will allow them to develop higher-order thinking skills. Some of the ways to actively engage students in the classroom after viewing lectures on video are as follows.

1. class discussions
2. debates
3. think-pair-share

4. cooperative learning
5. surveys and polls
6. graphing and displaying data
7. visual arts projects
8. low or high tech presentations
9. experiments
10. research projects

Unlike classroom lectures, online lessons can be reviewed from as far back as the beginning of the lesson if necessary. They can even be reviewed before major exams. Parents will love having the change in homework. Struggling through trying to work problems or answer questions about forgotten classroom lectures is eliminated. They can even view the videos themselves in order to be better able to help children understand the lesson content. Although the flipped classroom is relatively new, results of studies are showing improvements across the board from better test scores to lowered drop-out rates in schools that have implemented flipped instruction.

Final Thoughts on the Flipped Classroom

Have fun with this cool new idea. Start off slowly if you are "tech shy." Just remember the basic idea of the flipped classroom, and it will make sense. It could turn your teaching right side up and make more sense to you and your students. Flipping the classroom has transformed our teaching practice. We no longer stand in front of our students and talk at them for thirty to sixty minutes at a time. This radical change has allowed us to take on a different role with our students. Both of us taught for many years (a combined thirty-seven years) using this model. We were both good teachers. In fact, Jonathan received the Presidential Award for Excellence in Math and Science Teaching while being the sage on the stage, and Aaron received the same award under the Flipped model. Though as we look back, we could never go back to teaching in the traditional manner.

The flipped classroom has not only changed our classrooms, but many teachers from around the world have adopted the model and are using it to teach Spanish, Science, Math, elementary, middle, high school, and adults. We have presented all over North America and have seen how flipping your classroom can change kids' lives.

Flipping Increases Student Interaction

One of the greatest benefits of flipping is that overall interaction increases: Teacher to student and student to student. Since the role of the teacher has changed from presenter of content to learning coach, we spend our time talking to kids. We are answering questions, working with small groups, and guiding the learning of each student individually. When students are working on an assignment and we notice a group of students who are struggling with the same thing, we automatically organize the students into a tutorial group. We often conduct mini-lectures with groups of students who are struggling with the same content. The beauty of these mini-lectures is we are delivering "just in time" instruction when the students are ready for learning.

Since the role of the teacher has changed, to more of a tutor than a deliverer of content, we have the privilege of observing students interact with each other. As we roam around the class, we notice the students developing their own collaborative groups. Students are helping each other learn instead of relying on the teacher as the sole disseminator of knowledge. It truly is magical to observe. We are often in awe of how well our students work together and learn from each other.

Some might ask how we developed a culture of learning. We think the key is for students to identify learning as their goal, instead of striving for the completion of assignments. We have purposely tried to make our classes places where students carry out meaningful activities instead of completing busy work. When we respect our students in this way, they usually respond. They begin to realize, and for some it takes time, that we are here to guide them in their learning instead of being the authoritative pedagogue. Our goal is for them to be the best learner possible, and to truly understand the content in our classes. When our students grasp the concept that we are on their side, they respond by doing their best.

Flipping Changes the Way We Talk with Parents

We both remember sitting in parent conferences for years and parents would often ask us how their son or daughter behaved in class. What they were really asking was does my son or daughter sit quietly, act respectfully, raise their hand, and not disturb other students. These traits are certainly good for all to learn, but we struggled answering this question when we first started flipping the classroom. You see, the question is a non-issue in our classroom. Since students are coming with the primary focus on learning, the real question is now: Is your student learning or not? If they are not learning, what can we do to help them learn? This is a much more profound question and when we can discuss this with parents, we can really move students into a place which will help them become better learners. There are a myriad of reasons why a student is not learning well. Do students have some missing background knowledge? Do students have personal issues that interfere with their learning? Or are students more concerned with "playing school" rather than learning. When the parents and teachers can diagnose why the child is not learning we create a powerful moment where the necessary interventions can be implemented.

References

1. Alvarez, B. (2011). Flipping the classroom: homework in class, lessons at home. Learning First, Retrieved from http://www.learningfirst.org/flipping-classroom-homework-class-lessons-home

2. Bergmann, J.; Sams, A. (2008) Remixing chemistry class. *Learning and Leading with Technology.* 36(4) 24-27.

3. Berrett, D. (2012). How 'flipping' the classroom can improve the traditional lecture. *The Chronicle of Higher Education,* Retrieved from http://chronicle.com/article/How-Flipping-the-Classroom/130857/

4. Houston, M., & Lin, L. (2012, March). Humanizing the classroom by flipping the homework versus lecture equation. Paper presented at Society for information technology & teacher education international conference (site) 2012, Austin, TX.

5. Liles, M. (2012, April 10). [Web log message]. Retrieved from http://blog.discoveryeducation.com/blog/2012/04/10/flip-your-classroom-with-iscovery-education/

6. November, A. (2012). Flipped learning: a response to fie common criticisms. November Learning, Retrieved from http://novemberlearning.com/resources/archive-of-articles/flipped-learning-a-response-to-five-common-criticisms/

7. White, D. (2011). Literature justification for blended/reverse instruction. Unpublished raw data, Liberty University, Lynchburg, Virginia.

16

Blended Learning

Introduction

In a world of continuous change, few are confident enough to predict the future, yet the need to look ahead and prepare is vital. The objective of the paper is making the Gen Next as an employable generation through innovative educational methods like Blended Learning and thus preparing the generation ready for the Digital Age and era beyond the Digital Age. Though the conventional method of teaching process is useful and achieves its purpose, in the fast moving age the younger generation has to be more technical savvy. The new teaching learning process is the need of the hour and it will make the learners to gain confidence and make them employable to the core, anywhere in the world. Only when there is a rethinking in our approach in learning and education, we can enjoy the complete advantages of the new technologies.

The purpose of education is often considered as a "movement from dark to light", "ultimate change towards betterment "or" preparation for life", but, a content livelihood is the prime focus of education for any individual. Mere knowledge in the respective subject will seldom support one to get his dream job. An aspired livelihood can be achieved only when one is employed better. Employability skills will help one to be placed well. In the current Computer age, every profession, in one way or the other, is interlinked with digital technical knowledge. So, literacy in digital technology, employability skills, and a better livelihood are related to each other. "Tamil Nadu Teachers Education University" in its web page has proudly stated that it is in "pursuit of excellence in Promoting human values for social harmony and to make colleges of education excels through innovative teaching, research and extension activities." Yes, TNTEU University has futuristically foreseen the need of innovative teaching methods and hence emerges this subject of discussion.

The unique word "Employability" should have been coined from two words, Employee's and Ability. Employability, according to Manchester Metropolitan University, is, "the development of skills, abilities and personal attributes that students' capability to secure rewarding and satisfying outcomes in their economic, social and community lives."

Learning Computer as a subject or gaining computer skills through co curricular or extracurricular learning activities will not help one to attain Digital Fluency. The core method of teaching through Digital technology will for sure help the learners to gain digital literacy. More over Digital technology is not confined to computer alone. It has a vast area to cover, start from children's toy to satellite. So, the very teaching method for the next generation student must be through Digital Technology. Such learning process will instill the digital fluency within the learners in a subtle way.

One among the innovative way of digital learning process is "Blended Learning". It is a very unique and innovative method of learning practice, combining teaching methods both from face to face and online learning. Sometimes learning through face to face method and digital class room, it may not be online, but offline is too, termed as "Blended Learning". It meets all the expectations of 21st century learners in respect to efficiency, digital fluency, self learning opportunities, optimism, flexibility and personalization of students' learning experience, which makes them employable to the core. It is not of acquiring digital knowledge but learning every subject using and supported by the digital tools. The learners must be able to apply digital tools. Learning can happen through any digital method, visual, audio or textual mode.

Building Innovations

When creativity is thinking up new things, innovation is doing new things. Innovation follows creativity. Innovation's last phase is making invoices, as termed by the trading community. Ideas in paper are turned to be currencies in trade. But in field like education, innovation means much different. The institutions and policy makers aspire to utilize innovative ideas for the uplifting of humanity in all aspects. Considering the growth of the digital technology as well the expectations of the employers the learners of coming generation have to get updated to meet the job market requirements. Today's learners are the tomorrow's, executives, CEOs, labourers, teachers, entrepreneurs, policy makers and more. So, learning methods have to be innovative and creative to imbibe the required technical as well digital skills to the students.

Digital Literacy

In this digital age, our definition of literacy is changing completely. Now a day many jobs require a high level of IT competency and confidence. As such, the concept of Digital Literacy – those capabilities that equip an individual for living, learning and working in our IT-enabled society – is one that needs to be taken seriously by schools, colleges and universities, as well as by employers.

We live in an online and globally connected world. Society has a resulting need for citizens who can thrive in an era of digital information and communication. Those who are digitally literate are more likely to be economically secure, and these skills are especially important in higher education given that graduate jobs will almost invariably involve some level of contact with computers and portable devices. Against this backdrop, there is a clear need for education at all levels to play a part in establishing and developing the skills that the future employees will need.

At the same time, delivering digital literary goes beyond simply teaching the IT skills; a paradigm shift is required to live fully within the modern digital society, from understanding how to communicate ideas effectively in a range of media, to managing digital reputation and history, and understanding how to remain secure and protected throughout the process. Gone is the" Green Revolution" in agriculture which was an outcome of advances in Biotechnology and we are going to have a " Learning Revolution" in education, thanks to new Digital Technology.

Digital literacy gives young people the ability to take advantage of the wealth of new and emerging opportunities associated with digital technologies whilst also remaining alert to the various challenges technology can present.In fact, digital literacy is the 'savvyness' that allows young people to participate meaningfully and safely as digital technology becomes evermore pervasive in society.Schools are to be encouraged to embed the use of ICT in all subject areas of the primary and secondary curricula. Considering how digital literacy supports subject knowledge can help to ensure that technology-use enhances teaching and learning rather than simply becoming an add-on. Indeed, formal education must seek to prepare young people to make sense of the world and to thrive socially, intellectually and economically.

It can be said that digital media is now a central aspect of most people's lives, whatever their age.The skills, knowledge and understanding of digital literacy are therefore becoming indispensible as young people grow up in a society in which digital technology and media play an ever more important role. Digital technology makes the young people creative, and in return, the soceity becomes creative soceity.

Why learning through Digital mode in School Level?

Every third person in an Indian city today is a youth. By 2020, India is set to become the world's youngest country with 64 per cent of its population in the working age group. Quoting a report "The Hindu" newspaper says that the southern and western States will be the first to experience a growth dividend as they account for 63 per cent of all formally trained people. The largest share of youth with formal skills is found in Kerala, followed by Maharashtra, Tamil Nadu, Himachal Pradesh and Gujarat. The report finds that a person in an urban area has a 93 per cent greater chance of acquiring training than someone in a rural area. When the teaching pattern does consist uniform technology like Blended Learning, irrespective of territorial bindings and curriculum methods, the future generation will be more employable and well equipped to take up a career anywhere in the world.

The student population from rural India is in many fold in number than students from urban. They are the people, mostly first generation graduates of the family, who focus on IT and ITES careers. Thanks to MNCs which offer job scope for those students.In county like India, where majority of population live in villages, access to digital gadgets and opportunity to attain digital literacy is denied to every citizen.They dependent on schools and colleges for even to learn basic knowledge in computer. With the very basic skills in technology, they seldom get well paid career. But when the method of teaching itself is based on digital technology with Digital classrooms from the school level, it is easy for the rural students too to become fluent in digital technology.

Normally children arrive schools with basic knowledge of digital technology. It is not exaggerating if it is said that they come with their mobile phone or any other digital gadgets in hand to schools in urban India. When they are taught with black board or any other conventional method of teaching, it is not fair in the part of our educational system. They must be encouraged to enhance the skills they posses when they join the school. We say teacher is one who "Knows the way", "shows the way" and "goes the way". So, teaching all subjects through digital technology, like method of Blended Learning, will be interesting, easy to learn, as well they can attain digital fluency, in a professional manner. The level of motivation will be increased when they are taught through the mode they are familiar with.

Employability and Employable Generation

The term "Employability "can be defined in multiple ways according to the need of the industry, expectations of individuals and society. Employability in the words of Professor Mantz Yorke," is a set of achievements – skills, understandings and personal attributes – that make graduates more likely to gain employment and be successful in their chosen occupations, which benefits themselves, the workforce, the community and the economy".

It is estimated that around 90% of all new graduate jobs in United Kingdom require a high level of digital skills. Though it is the status in UK, it is the global demand. It will not take years for India to get the same scenario. So, the policy makers and educational institutions must focus on creating an Employable Generation rather than focusing on instilling employability skills in the learners.

Current status of the Job Seekers

Surveys on the employability skills of Indian graduates, graduated in any field of study, say, most of the job seekers are not employable in medium and high profile careers. They are not good in communication skills, don't have sufficient digital literacy and other core requirements for a good profile jobs. Neither Indian companies nor MNCs will employ them without a basic training. It is understood more number of trainees are rejected during the training pcriod itself. Such happenings make the rejected hands feel dejected and they think their future is dark. It is the status in all the field of study, like, management, technical and even in teaching profession.

The learners are not the only reason for such adverse scenario but the system we follow too plays major and vital role in this. So, to make our future generation employable we need a system which makes the learner master in all the fields required by the employers.

Blended Learning

"Teaching in the Internet age means we must teach tomorrow's skills today." Jennifer Fleming. "Preparing for future" can be termed as *motto* of Blended Learning. Though there are other new age teaching concepts like Flipped class rooms, Learning without Limits, Cloud Computing , Blended Leaning seems to be more innovative since it not only a blend of technologies but also a perfect blend of Traditional method of class room as well a New Age class room.

Blended learning, where multiple learning environments and activities are combined is a decades' old innovative concept of teaching. But contemporary definitions of blended learning take into account that technology can play more. Current as well futuristic concept of blended learning represents a combination of online and face to face experiences. It is the best of both worlds.

Blended learning is a student-centered approach to creating a learning experience whereby the learner interacts with other students, with the instructor, and with content through thoughtful integration of online and face-to-face environments. Some time Blended Learning consists of face to face instruction and usage of off line Digital tools instead of on line lessons.

In contrast to teacher-centered, rote-learning approaches, blended learning environments provide multiple ways to access content and to demonstrate mastery. As a result, they lend themselves more readily to differentiation of content and process. A blended approach also gives the learner the opportunity to be more responsible for his or her learning, which creates a learning situation that may be more meaningful on an individual level. Because the learner comes to construct knowledge through personal effort, she or he is more likely to demonstrate understanding beyond rote memorization, and to transfer what she or he has learned to new settings.

Blended Learning – An inevitable Teaching Method

India is a country which had more effective and traditional teaching methods like *Gurukula* method. Though it was age old, it has its own value and we respect such methods as they were man making way of teaching. Having such great methods of teaching we need not have to switch over entirely to complete online method of teaching process. Our culture respects *Guru* as father, mother, guide and God. Our *Vedas, Upanishads, Epics* like *Mahabharata and Ramayana,* master pieces like *Thirukural* always speak high and great of Gurus. None other country gives this much respect and high regard to *Guru,* the teacher. Still our education system mostly depends on teachers. We, Indians give more importance to moral and man making education than attaining mass production of graduates. In this back drop, it is difficult to imagine teaching without a teacher or learning without a Guru.

In this digital era, traditional classroom teaching methods are not much effective to achieve current learning standards. Technological approaches alone can't provide students with deep and meaningful learning experience. But the combination of both, say, Blended Learning and face to face teaching can help an individual to attain moral values, command over the subject as well digital fluency. Such an employee with a multiple skills, moral values, digital literacy and adaptability is most wanted by the employers and in coming years, they are the only preferred hands by employers in any field and anywhere in the world. So, for country like ours, Blended Learning could be the most apt mode of teaching, where we have face to face instruction and technology based learning. In this method of learning, the learners will have a personal touch with the teachers as well they are independent in learning. It could be a perfect blend of modern and traditional ways of learning.

Getting blended is vital at this moment. Blended learning is more than electronic textbooks and productivity tools. It means inventing or adopting new learning environments that work better for students as well teachers. It increases opportunities for students to engage with technology such as teacher using digital class rooms, a school computer lab, and computers using digital curriculum in the class rooms are more supportive for the learners to attain digital literacy and to get the dream jobs in future. Clearly there are more opportunities for exploration and growth in the use of blended learning from the school level. Some of this growth may be driven by increasing student demands for more learning process.

Acting Independently With the Digital Technology

Motivation is the driving force for success. The learners have to have a change in their attitude to be taught through a different mode of teaching method, an innovative method. They may feel fish out of water in digital class room and it may be very difficult for them to come out of comfort zone, an accustomed zone of conventional mortar class room learning. When they are motivated they will readily open their mind for new learning. Yes, mind is like a parachute, it works only when it is open. It is in the hands of the teachers to make them to understand the dire need of the change of learning which is going to make them employable. Lot of comparisons can be sited from other countries and cultures to make them to realise the value of the Blended Learning. Even they can be asked to prepare papers supporting the idea. Discussions can be arranged to speak for and against the concept where their eyes can be opened.

Getting Accustomed in Handling Digital Tools

It is very vital stage of learning process. Students from rural areas usually will have a pessimistic attitude towards digital tools. It must be taken care that they must not keep aloof in the class rooms and it can be monitored no inferiority complex comes in learners from rural areas. Slowly the digital tools can be introduced to the learners and till they feel free in handling the tools they must be free from core teaching.

Creating Awareness of Technicalities of the Digital Tools

Simply using the digital tools will not help the learners to attain expertise in the field. Apart from software knowledge they must have the basic hardware skills too. It will help them to become an all rounder in his field. So, basic technicalities of the digital tools can be taught to the learners. It is like car drivers knowing the mechanism of the car, which will help them to attend the faults in the machine, complete his journey successfully even after break downs.

Using the Digital Tools for Communication and Learning Purpose

Once they are motivated and aware of the importance and

necessity of the blended learning, accustomed in handling the digital tools and acquire hardware skills, it is right time for them to be introduced to proper and fully fledged learning. The regular subjects will be taught through the blended learning method. Face to face as well online and off line classes will be given. They will gain confident towards the teachers and the new method of learning. Apart from regular subjects they must use the digital tools for communication purpose too.

Acting Independently With the Digital Tools

This is the last phase in Blended Learning. It is an assessment of their learning. Seminars, symposiums, conferences can be conducted in this phase. The learner becomes a teacher now. They can be asked to handle classes for their peer group using the digital tools. Question answer sessions, group discussions on their respective subjects can be arranged in which the Blended Learning pattern can be followed. When they act independently they get confidence in their related subjects as well they feel good and positive in using the digital tools for all purpose.

Conclusion

To conclude, a survey conducted in America can be sited which has found that college students prefer blended learning course over those that are solely face to face or solely online. This is the scenario everywhere in the world. "We need to give people a new set of skills in an explicit way that will make them more marketable for the job market", foresees Cristina Costa. Yes, by providing relevant and authentic learning experiences that offer opportunities to develop and evidence professional practice not only enhances student employability but also more importantly makes good business sense for colleges and universities, for employers and for the economy as a whole.

Normally computers are used as source centre of information and the learners are taught how to browse, send E-mails, know to work in word or excel. But the learners must become fluent with computer so that they can create and express instead passing information. To help the learners to attain Digital Fluency, the mode of teaching must be an innovative one. Among all other technology based teaching methods Blended Learning will be an opt one for our country. When the forth coming age is going to be a Digital Age, the job aspirants must be a computer literate. Any knowledge the learners get learning computer through extracurricular or co curricular activities will make them aware of computers not expert in it. They can access computer, but they cannot express. They can play for lifelong but cannot make it as bread winner. Shortly, it can be said Blended Learning which is a holistic approach to technology enhanced learning will make the new generation learners employable and we can have an employable generation on the other hand.

References

1. Careers & Employability Service, www.mmu.ac.uk/careers/guides , Manchester Metropolitan University
2. Learning & Employability – Series One – Employability in higher education: what it is - what it is not – By Mantz Yorke, published by The Higher Education Academy, Innovation Way, York Science Park, Heslington, York, UK.
3. Race Online 2012:www.raceonline2012.org/stories/jobcentre-plus
4. The Hindu, April 17th 2013. Online edition, www.thehindu.com
5. Cristina Costa, Research Technologies Development Officer, Research and Graduate College, University of
6. Echo360 2012 student survey, "Blended Learning Technology: Connecting with the Online-All-the-Time
7. Student," www.echo360.com/studentsurveys Ibid

17

Cloud Computing in Higher Education

Introduction

In the current financial crisis, educational institutions and universities are facing difficulties in providing necessary support for educational, research and development activities. Cloud computing is the alternative to address the issues there by improving agility and obtain savings. Cloud computing is an emerging area which can be used for sharing the resources with the help of web technology like Software as a Service (SaaS), Platform as a Service (PaaS) and Infrastructure as a Service (IaaS). Practically Cloud Computing is extension of Grid computing with independency and smarter tools and technological gradients. Healthy Cloud Computing helps in sharing of software, hardware, application and other packages with the help of internet tools and wireless media. Cloud computing can be a welcomed optioned in the universities and educational institutes for higher studies. And also the educational institutes, universities and industries are playing vital role in transforming the society and entire world economy. Various researches are carried out to update the present IT infrastructure especially in the area of education.

Cloud computing provides shared resources, software and information through Internet as a PAYGO (Pay-as-you-go) basis. Cloud Computing is a kind of virtualization; thus also known as Virtualization Technology. Cloud Computing and its benefits attracts several other field. Education Systems also interacts with Educational applications for Cloud Computing. Cloud Computing provides several benefits in Educational Systems such as creation of Virtual teaching learning environment, making interacting and speedy smart class room, it also minimizes the time of knowledge collection model preparation and delivery. Cloud Computing and its benefits are used around the world and especially in the Western countries. Due to poverty and underdevelopment; Asian and African and other undeveloped countries are still unable to offer such benefits to teachers, student, administrator, instructor and other stakeholders related to education systems. The challenges and issues are one of the important concerns for strong and healthy educational systems powered by cloud computing and virtualization technique.

Higher Education

Higher education was acknowledged in time as one of the pillars of society development. Through the partnerships between universities, government and industry, researchers and students have proven their contribution to the transformation of society and the entire world economy. The tendency observed during the last few years within the higher education level is the universities' transition to research universities and ongoing update of the IT (Information Technology) infrastructure as foundation for educational activities and Science research.

With the evolution of technology, the number of services which migrate from traditional form to the online form grows as well.

For these specific services, an adequate providing form must be found in the online environment, using the proper technologies, guaranteeing the access of large number of users, fast and secure services. Due to this aspect, at the moment universities are confronting with a dramatic increase of costs in higher education, more than the inflation rate and a decrease of universities' budgets, which leads to the pressure of finding some alternative means of reaching their purpose i.e. the education of students and accomplishing the research.

Cloud Computing (CC)

Cloud Computing is a new technology which is an improvement of distributed computing, parallel computing and grid computing. The basic principle of cloud computing is making tasks distributed among large number of computers but not in local computers or remote servers. This is a dynamic model, based on pay-per-use (subscription) or scalable system in which configuration of resources (hardware, platform/services) can be graded to suit the needs of the users for optimum utilization of resources. In simple words, it is a subscription- based or pay-per-use real time service over the internet.

The following **National Institute of Standards and Technology (NIST)** definitions are used for deployment models:

Private cloud The cloud infrastructure is operated solely for an organization. It may be managed by the organization or a third party and may exist on premise or off premise.

Community cloud The cloud infrastructure is shared by several organizations and supports a specific community that has shared concerns (e.g., mission, security requirements, policy, and compliance considerations). It may be managed by the organizations or a third party and may exist on premise or off premise.

Public cloud The cloud infrastructure is made available to the general public or a large industry group and is owned by an organization selling cloud services.

Hybrid cloud The cloud infrastructure is a composition of two or more clouds (private, community, or public) that remain unique entities but are bound together by standardized or proprietary technology that enables data and application portability (e.g., cloud bursting for load balancing between clouds).

Characteristics of Cloud Computing

There are many distinguishing features of cloud computing but some important features are.

(a) Versatility
(b) Cost-effectiveness (pay-per-use)
(c) Virtualization
(d) Security
(e) Sustainability
(f) Scalability
(g) User-friendly
(h) Resource Optimisation
(i) Infrastructure and service-level agreements (SLAs)

Types of Cloud Computing

The following is a list of the three main types of services that can be offered by the cloud:

1. Software as a Service (SaaS): The applications, such as e-mail, people use every day.
2. Platform as a Service (PaaS): The operating environment in which applications run.
3. Infrastructure as a Service (IaaS): The on-demand data centers.

Outsourcing some capabilities to the cloud makes the most of what's on-site by freeing time, budget, and people. For example, with SaaS, you can add services, like e-mail, affordably. With PaaS, you can deliver services broadly without having to manage the infrastructure. With IaaS, you get pay-as-you-go data center capacity for adding CPUs, storage, networking, or Web hosting. Take, for example, a typical university with an IT infrastructure that caters for the needs of students, teaching staff and management, research staff and software developers (e.g., Web developers).

Demand for IT services in this environment is directed to the IT Services Department whose job is to:

- provide students and staff with software (e.g., email accounts, operating systems, productivity applications, malware detectors and cleaners, etc.) and hardware (e.g., PCs, Servers, etc.);
- provide researchers and postgraduate students with the required special software and hardware to run experiments that are likely to involve a great deal of processing and computation;
- provide Web developers with the development tools needed to write and host Web applications.

Many aspects of this arrangement can be migrated to the cloud. For example, students, administrative staff and lecturers can be made to use the services of providers of SaaS and IaaS clouds. These services will be ideally accessed through thin clients. Any software launched by these groups of people resides on the servers of the SaaS cloud provider and is accessed online.

A growing number of academic institutions are turning to SaaS for their desktop applications. For example, Madras University uses an e-mail solution hosted in the cloud. Students now have the free collaboration tools they want, people on campus have the tools they need to work together, and administrators are finding it easier and more cost-effective to manage.

SaaS for education: Microsoft Live@edu

Microsoft Live@edu is a program that provides students, staff, faculty, and alumni long-term, primary e-mail addresses and other applications that they can use to collaborate and communicate online—all at no cost to education institutions. Students will be using Microsoft products similar to those used in many workplaces that help to prepare them for jobs after college.

Cloud computing initiatives

There are good number of cloud computing initiatives undertaken by Amazon, Google, Microsoft and others offering various types of cloud computing services for the organizations, businesses, and individuals. IBM Cloud Academy, IEEE Cloud Computing initiatives are offered some services in Education.

IBM Cloud Academy

IBM (International Business Machines) launched the IBM Cloud Academy (2009), a global forum for educators, researchers and information technology (IT) personnel from the education industry to pursue cloud computing initiatives, develop skills and share best practices for reducing operating costs while improving quality and access to education.

IEEE Cloud Computing

The IEEE (Institute of Electrical and Electronics Engineers) Cloud Computing Initiative represents the first, broad-based collaborative endeavor for cloud computing to be offered by a global technical professional organization. Six interdependent activity tracks are included in the IEEE Cloud Computing Initiative: the

Web portal; conferences; continuing education courses; publications; standards development; and a test bed to be used in the development of cloud standards and applications as well as for education and research.

Amazon Web Services (AWS)

Amazon is perceived as one of the major players in the business, offering a wide range of prominent cloud computing services such as elastic compute cloud (EC2), simple storage service (S3), simple DB and simple queuing service (SQS). It provides a reliable, scalable, low-cost infrastructure platform in the cloud that powers hundreds of thousands of businesses in countries around the world. Some of the solutions offered by Amazon through cloud computing include application hosting, web hosting, backup and storage, enterprise IT, content delivery, and database.

Google Apps

Google Apps cloud services, a multi-tenant, and internet-scale infrastructure, offers faster access to innovation, superior reliability, and security, and maximum economies of scale as compared to on-premises, hosted and software plus services technologies8. Google Apps is available free for individuals and organizations (limited up to 10 user accounts), educational institutions and US non-profitable organizations and for a price to businesses and organizations.

Microsoft Windows Azure

Microsoft is also investing heavily in this new computing service delivery model and has introduced Azure, as its cloud offering. Azure has three components: Windows Azure (which provides developers with on-demand compute and storage to host, scale, and manage Internet or cloud applications), SQL Azure (which extends the capabilities of Microsoft SQL Server into the cloud as a Web-based distributed relational database) and Azure .Net Services (which include a set of Microsoft-hosted, highly scalable, developer-oriented services that provide key building blocks required by many cloud-based and cloud-aware applications).

Education and the Cloud Computing

Colleges and universities are always on the lookout to upgrade their software and IT hardware in order to attract students and keep pace with the rapid developments in digital technologies. Cloud computing could provide those institutions with the means to achieve those ambitions at prices they can afford. Furthermore, shifting responsibility to external providers for managing some aspects of their software and hardware infrastructures could also result in cost savings with relation to labor, as fewer IT services staff will be needed than before. Cloud Computing is gaining popularity in educational systems, especially in online education and corporate education; E-Learning is gaining popularity through web 2.0 platform of Cloud Computing ; Still in India, higher educational institutes are not moving towards healthy Cloud Computing solutions; Governmental grants, non availability of software and packages related to educational field are important issues.

1. The online and e-learning systems may gain rapidly with the help of Cloud Computing; the aspects such as online question paper distribution, paper collection, full text book and module delivery is possible with Cloud Computing.
2. Social Computing such as Social 2.0 powered web technologies is also a kind of Cloud Computing; which allows sharing of educational data, text, notes and recorded video without extra support. The challenges of such systems are mainly people awareness, student awareness, teachers and faculty towards sharing and creation of group of

learner. Many teachers and students may not aware about IT and Social Networking usages.

3. Creation of smart class room, online and continuing education university education has come to the door step of learner. Here Cloud Computing is used in several cases.
4. More importantly, Cloud Computing based education systems saves cost by centralized IT Infrastructure, rapid transfer, elasticity, flexibility and other benefits in education
5. Cloud computing also promotes some new educational mode such as-corporate learning, industry integrated learning programme; where students get knowledge and classes from online media in his/her office or corporate house. It is helpful for the working students. But for that a mutual understanding between education service provider and corporate agency is essential. The main reason behind this is, space for projection, tools and technological and electricity support and so on.

Advantages of Cloud Computing

1. There is no need to own all infrastructure facilities as cloud computing takes care of it.
2. With the help of Broadband and healthy connection anywhere and anytime services are possible;
3. It provides large amounts of processing power comparable to supercomputer level.
4. It provides an effective and creative service delivery model;
5. Cloud Computing model does not support any long term commitments.
6. Capital expenditure is minimized

A convenient tool to engage in the scholarship of teaching and learning.

Cloud Computing Based Education: Challenges and Issues

Many challenges of cloud computing for higher education relate to its relative newness and the underdevelopment of the marketplace for cloud services. For higher education, decisions to adopt cloud computing will be influenced by more than technical and cost considerations.

Information is the lifeblood of higher education, and decisions on how to manage that information can have far-reaching political, social, and economic considerations. Adoption of cloud computing presents many of the same risks and challenges as deciding to use a more traditional outsourcing arrangement. The increased possibility that the service provider or its resources may reside outside of a government's legal or territorial jurisdiction, however, can make some of these concerns more acute. At present, as many universities are trying to update their IT infrastructure and data, but they are facing few challenges which can be solved by cloud computing. The challenges are as follows:

1. **Cost**: choose the subscription or PAYGO plan.

2. **Flexibility**: cloud computing allows to dynamically scale the investment in infrastructures as demand fluctuate.

3. **Accessibility**: making the data and services available publicly without losing the sensitive information

4. **Security**: making data secure.

Conclusion

Cloud computing is a new baby in the computer systems technology emerged owing to the developments in internet and associated technologies. It is in the evolving stage, requires some amount of careful considerations before organizations think about hosting some of their services. E-Learning or online education is need of hour. Today several modes of education have originated with the help of IT and computing. It provides several opportunities; Cloud Computing plays an important role for overall IT infrastructure development. Regular education may also benefit from Cloud Computing. The small room, mobile based education is the wonderful gift of IT and especially Cloud Computing. Universities, Engineering colleges, and other higher educational institutes should go for Cloud Computing and virtualization. Proper funding and planning are essential for healthy Cloud Computing packages. Proper and adequate training programme on Cloud Computing need to be introduced.

Reference

1. Aladwani, Adel M,(2002) "An integrated performance model of information systems projects", *Journal of Management Information Systems*, 19(1).
2. AbdulKalam, APJ (2003) "IT Strategy in Defense Environment", DESIDOC *Bulletin of Information Technology*, 20(1 & 2): 7-12.
3. Bates, M (1990) "Where should the person stop and the information search interface start?' *Information Processing & Management*, 26(5): 575–591.
4. Belkin, N. J., & Robertson, S.E. (1976) "Information science and the phenomena of information." *Journal of the American Society for Information Science*, 27(4):197–204.
5. Denning, P. J., & et al. (1989) Computing as a discipline. *Communication of the ACM*, 32(1),23.
6. Dhawan, Neelam (2011) Cloud computing can counter illiteracy. *Times of India*,

7. Fox, A. (2009) Cloud computing in education. *Berkeley iNews*, https://inews. B erkeley.edu/articles/ Spring2009/cloud-computing

8. Hayes, B. (2008) Cloud computing. *Communications of ACM*, 51(7): 9-11.

9. Scale, Mark-Shane E (2009) Cloud computing and collaboration. *Library Hi Tech News*, 26(9): 10-13.

10. Wikipedia. Cloud computing. http://en.wikipedia.org/ wiki/Cloud computing.

18

Effective Academic Excellence

Introduction

Education plays a very significant role in developing an individual to his full potential by bringing out his latent talents and nurturing them. The forces of environment begin to influence the growth and development of the individual right from the womb of the mother. A proper and adequate environment is very much necessary for a fruitful learning of the child. In recent years, we have witnessed rapid social and cultural changes, phenomenal advances in communication and information technologies, as well as the introduction of the Internet within schools. These factors have contributed to shape the teaching and operating cultures of schools and created shifts in our expectations of the physical learning environment. They have affected teachers, educators and researchers the world over. These miniature revolutions have given rise to an urgent need for a new generation of facilities to cater for 21st century teaching and learning needs. Good learning environment is one in which staff, students and, parents build safe and peaceful environment where people feel accepted and respected and where learning is the main focus. Therefore a positive learning environment where all students feel comfortable, wanted, valued, accepted, and secure must be created. The use of innovative methods in educational institutions has the potential not only to improve education, but also to empower people, strengthen governance and galvanize the effort to achieve the human development goal for the country. The present paper deals with the effective, appropriate and interactive use of computer – related technologies for designing learning environment of tomorrow which induce and pave ways for academic excellence.

Education plays a very significant role in developing an individual to his full potential by bringing out his latent talents and nurturing them. Education shapes a person. According to Dewey 'Education is a continuous process of experiencing and of revising or non-revising experiences. It is the development of all those capacities in the individual, which enables him to control his environment and fulfill his possibilities'. The forces of environment begin to influence the growth and development of the individual right from the womb of the mother. A proper and adequate environment is very much necessary for a fruitful learning of the child. Especially the school and home should provide the necessary stimulus for learning experience. In recent years, we have witnessed rapid social and cultural changes, phenomenal advances in communication and information technologies, as well as the introduction of the Internet within schools. These factors have contributed to shape the teaching and operating cultures of schools and created shifts in our expectations of the physical learning environment. They have affected teachers, educators and researchers the world over. These miniature revolutions have given rise to an urgent need for a new generation of facilities to cater for 21st century teaching and learning needs. Good learning environment is one in which staff, students and, parents build safe and peaceful environment where people feel accepted and respected and where learning is the main focus. Therefore a learning environment, where all students feel comfortable, wanted, valued, accepted, and secure, must be created.

A positive school climate affects everyone associated with the school, be it the students, staff, parents, and the community. Improved school climate is a goal to pursue. Educators need to constant up work towards improving their school climate, culture, and conditions to that students learning is improved. The world could be synchronized with the development of science and technology. Education is the means for all these developments. Education is the essence of every civilization. The use of innovative methods in educational institutions has the potential not only to improve education, but also to empower people, strengthen governance and galvanize the effort to achieve the human development goal for the country.

Conceptual Framework

Learning takes place effectively only when proper and congenial environment is provided for children. Positive learning environment exists when all students feel comfortable, wanted, valued, accepted, and secure in an environment where they trust. Many of the modern learning environments being built today promote and support a range of pedagogies including delivering, applying, creating, communicating and decision-making. Modern learning environments support strengths-based teaching and can offer students and teachers flexibility, openness and access to resources. Providing teachers with an open, flexible learning environment can lead to the development of a robust, continuously improving community of practice.

Learning environment should support multiple perspective or interpretations of reality, knowledge construction, and experience based activities. In the age of globalization the modern computer – related technologies help in changing the learning environment rapidly and make the pedagogy more and more interactive. With the use of computer technology, classroom learning process tends to accelerate day by day. Computer technologies increase the level of teaching and motivate students to provide information in an interesting and innovative way by making teaching more and more effective. The appropriate and effective use of technology facilitates to gain information in depth. The present paper deals with the effective, appropriate and interactive use of computer – related technologies for designing learning environment of tomorrow which induce and pave ways for academic excellence.

Computer – assisted learning provides a huge amount of information to the learners in a short period of time. Learners are reinforced in a powerful way through the medium of discussion in classroom. It helps in stimulating the students to learn through the use of multimedia, provides students different varieties of information, provides more powerful ICT tools for problem solving and learning and allows the students to work at their pace. Every learner should not only be a computer literate but also develop competencies in the effective usage of computers and all the technologies that are related to learning, Age –old method of chalk and talk in classroom should be dead and gone.

Changing the learning process:

In the late '90s' many in the education field and government, as well as in the media and public, recognized a 'digital divide' in which some school districts and classrooms were "wired" and had up-to-date computer technology, while others did not, Accordingly, there were efforts undertaken by government, business and educators to wire classrooms and make computer technology available to a greater number of students and teachers. While many teachers and students are engaging in innovative forms of research and novel projects, there are still many traditional teachers who resist learning new computer skills and do not want to bring computer- based technologies into their classrooms

Teachers have to develop the ability to demonstrate how these technologies can be used for academic purposes and convey the educational advantages of computers and the Internet to their students. This means acquiring and teaching new literacy involving teachers and students in innovative types of research projects, and interacting in novel ways as everyone learns to use new technology and media.

Indeed, to meet the challenges of an always- evolving high-tech society, teachers today need to develop multiple forms of computer and information literacy to help improve education. This means using technology in the classroom to illustrate lesson topics; teaching students how to use the Internet and information technology to research topics; and using technology to enhance education outside the classroom, ideally in the ways that involve students in the learning process.

Teachers might share large learning spaces, rather than traditional classrooms, with children at different levels, learning different things. Classroom design developments include flexible teaching spaces that can be expanded or reduced in size depending on what's being taught and what technology requirements are needed. Some modern options include hexagonal shapes with a shared common centre area, and outdoor areas and decking off each learning space. Sliding glass walls can be used to open up or close down spaces providing both flexibility and an open, bright environment. Specialist equipment within a school can be shared by all, and with the wider community. This could be a fully-fitted industrial kitchen, or a modern science laboratory lined with wall-to-wall glass that allows other students to walk past and observe what's going on. Whole walls can be whiteboard, or white-boards can be movable. Teachers can opt to change the way the class is facing, or break children up into groups.

The key principles of Learning Environment of Tomorrow

Flexibility

Creating flexible spaces that accommodate a wide range of current and future teaching and learning styles is the key. While we cannot anticipate all of the future needs for educational facilities we can know with certainty that they will change. Teaching spaces that can be adapted and support the educational agility of teachers and students will be an environment that can deliver outstanding educational outcomes. We should not get stuck with replicating 'business as usual' solutions when we could have spaces that support innovation and creative learning.

The Learning Community

The modern learning environment can gain significant benefits from being designed for the community it serves. While funding is a one-size-fits-all model, the project team can actually deliver a project that reflects and supports the wider school community. And when a school is designed as a learning community it is a powerful way to engage with students, staff and parents.

Classroom / Learning Studio

A classroom can offer so much more when combined with other spaces such as small seminar or breakout rooms, group learning areas or even external learning decks can offer the opportunity for a wide variety of learning styles. Adjacencies and visibility are so important in making this work well.

Group Learning Areas

Group learning spaces can take over from the corridor for circulation but also create wonderful opportunities for teaching and learning at different scales – from small groups or combined classes. They can also be a powerful physical manifestation of the learning community described above, and surrounded by visible learning studios and small seminar / breakout rooms they support the flexible, agile leaning of the future.

Outdoor Learning Environment

Often the external spaces for the school are an afterthought and yet they represent a fantastic opportunity to create great learning spaces. The key is visibility. The power of passive surveillance through being able to remotely supervise a space through good visibility can transform behaviours and learning outcomes. Careful thought by designers can unlock the potential of the neglected areas in your school grounds, bringing them back into the overall learning environment. School buildings should support and inspire the wonderful learning opportunities that can happen in and around them.

Learning environment of tomorrow must encompass a holistic approach that relates the pedagogy of learning to the physical and virtual spaces in which learning occurs. Each of the following characteristics can pose to design a learning environment of tomorrow:

1. a dynamic transformative learning centre that provides a welcoming, vibrant and culturally inclusive environment
2. a place of awe and enchantment, exploration and curiosity
3. a large, flexible learning space based on fluid design principles
4. a space that includes print, e-resources, and multi-media, and provides access to a range of ICT hardware and software fully supported by robust ICT infrastructure

Functional elements within a learning environment of tomorrow

1. Enable learning to be demonstrated by students participating, reading, watching, publishing, creating, researching, and performing in groups or individually.
2. Have flexible spaces that can be adapted for individual, small or large group use with acoustic considerations. This will allow students to work individually, to reflect, as well as collaborate on projects, and discuss and share ideas.
3. Have interiors designed using modular, flexible, multi-use furniture. Power points will be installed everywhere and offer charging for mobile learning devices.

For augmenting and strengthening the use of innovative strategies in the classrooms of India, we need to work on the following areas:

1. Curricular reforms
2. Faculty development
3. Academic leadership
4. Renewal of Higher Quality standards
5. E-skill development
6. Adopting the under privileged or Rural villages
7. Professional competence.

Conclusion

Academic excellence is one of the most important goals of education. It can be defined as excellence in all disciplines. It encompasses student ability and performance. The effective growth and development, the desirable learning experiences, attitudes and values to be developed in the child depends upon the main factor learning environment. The study demands the designing of learning environment of tomorrow. Further the educational resources and infrastructure needs to be updated in rural schools so that the academic excellence can be uplifted in such schools.

References

1. Dillenbourg, Pierre. "Virtual learning environments" (PDF). EUN Conference 2000: Learning in the new millennium: Building new education strategies for schools

2. Dinesh Kumar, Amit Singh. Computer technology as an interactive teaching system a new trend in education, Edutrack, January 2013, Vol.12, No: 5.

3. G. Kearsley and B. Shneiderman, 'Engagement theory: A framework for technology-based teaching and learning', Educational Technology, 38, 5 (September-October 1998), pp. 20-23. accessed as http://home.sprynet.com/~gkearsley/engage.htm on 21 February 2000

4. G.Madhavi, N. Ramnath Kishan. Development of positive learning environment, Edutrack, November 2012, Vol.9, No: 3.

5. Jagannath.K, Dange, Praveen.R. Online learning a new way of education, Edutrack, July 2009, Vol.8, No: 11.

6. M. J. Stiles, 'Developing Tacit and Codified Knowledge and Subject Culture within a Virtual Learning Environment', IJEEE, 37, No1 (January 2000) pp 13-25

7. Moult, R. R. (2005), Learning to listen: Using ICT to capture pupils' perceptions and help the teacher to respond (PDF), p. 19.

8. Pea & K. Sheingold (Eds.), Mirrors of minds: Patterns of experience in educational computing (pp. 147-177). Norwood, NJ: Ablex Publishing

9. Pea, R. D., & Kurland, D. M. (1987). On the cognitive effects of learning computer programming. In R. D.

10. Puneet,Rahi.Innovations in teaching learning, Edutrack, July 2012, Vol.11, No: 11.

11. Seale, J (2009), A Research Briefing by the Technology Enhanced Learning Phase of the Teaching and Learning Research Programme (PDF).

12. Weller, M. (2007), Virtual Learning Environments: Using, choosing and developing your VLE, London: Routledge.

13. *Modern Learning Environments*, by Mark Osborne (PDF, 3.1mb)

19

Blended Learning

Introduction

Blended Learning refers to a mixing of different learning environments. Blended learning gives learners and teachers a potential environment to learn and teach more effectively. Our Blended Learning approach to instruction stems from the best practices, research, and experience available in the field of education today. We developed our revolutionary approach because we know that children learn best when exposed to different methods and approaches to instruction. The blended approach to instruction has seen a steady increase in the past years, and survey data indicates that administrators in higher education expect that trend to continue. An instructor can begin a course with a well-structured introductory lesson in the classroom, and then proceed with follow-up materials online. Blended learning can also be applied to the integration of e-learning with a Learning Management System using computers in a physical classroom, along with face-to-face instruction

Guidance is suggested early in the process, to be used more sparingly as learners gain expertise.

Blended Learning refers to a mixing of different learning environments. The phrase has many specific meanings based upon the context in which it is used. Blended learning gives learners and teachers a potential environment to learn and teach more effectively.

Whether a course should be proposed as a face-to-face interaction, an online course or a blended course depends on the analysis of the competences at stake, the nature and location of the audience, and the resources available. Depending on the cross-analysis of these 3 parameters, the course designer will opt for one of the 3 options. In his course scenario he/she will then have to decide which parts are online, which parts are offline. A basic example of this is a course of English as a second language where the instructor reaches the conclusion that all audio-based activities (listening comprehension, oral expression) will take place in the classroom where all text-based activities will take place online (reading comprehension, essays writing).

Blended learning increases the options for greater quality and quantity of human interaction in a learning environment. Blended learning offers learners the opportunity "to be both together and apart." A community of learners can interact at anytime and anywhere because of the benefits that computer-mediated educational tools provide. Blended learning provides a 'good' mix of technologies and interactions, resulting in a socially supported, constructive, learning experience; this is especially significant given the profound effect that it could have on distance learning.

Blended Learning is learning which combines online and face-to-face approaches. The following material resulted from an ANTA-funded project which set out to investigate blended learning through a series of interviews with teachers. A blended learning program uses a combination of e-learning and classroom instruction. Independent schools that teach English as a second language and TOEFL / TOEIC prep are using this learning solution to save time, lower costs, and improve quality of service to students.

Kaplan, one of the world's largest private education providers, sees blended learning as an essential part of its business strategy: Our Blended Learning approach to instruction stems from the best practices, research, and experience available in the field of education today. We developed our revolutionary approach because we know that children learn best when exposed to different methods and approaches to instruction.

Defining Blended Learning

There are brick and mortar options, such as coaching, classes, and mentoring. Then there are electronic options, ranging from e-learning classes, to on-line help systems, to templates, decision support tools, and knowledge bases. E-learning gurus Elliot Maisie and Brandon Hall recognize the many options and encourages combined systems, which they call 'brick and click,' or 'blended' learning" (Rossett & Sheldon, 2001).

Blended Learning can combine the positive aspects of the two learning environments, classroom-based learning and e-Learning (Bonk & Graham, 2006). However, some experts are now taking a broader view in that it goes beyond elearning and classrooms:

Blended learning is a mix of delivery methods that have been selected and fashioned to accommodate the various learning needs of a diverse audience in a variety of subjects. This method can include any combination of any of the above delivery methods (McSporran & King 2002).

'The integrated combination of traditional learning with web based on-line approaches'. This is, arguably, the classic definition of the term. 'Traditional learning' here is classroom teaching or 'face-to-face' language lessons. The delivery of the online part of the course is usually through learning technologies, typically involving a Virtual Learning Environment (VLE) such as 'Blackboard' or 'Moodle' and comprising the use of synchronous and asynchronous electronic tools, such as, respectively, 'chat' and 'bulletin boards'.

'The combination of media and tools employed in an e-learning environment'. This definition could describe a purely distance learning course, where no face-to-face lessons occur. Communication between the learner and e-tutor may take place through any number of technologies, such as email and internet telephone. 'The combination of a number of pedagogic approaches, irrespective of the learning technology used'. A course that combines 'transmission' and 'constructivist' approaches would fit into this category, such as one involving elements of a present-practice-produce methodology as well as task-based learning.

The term continues to develop. A further possible conceptualization of BL is as 'a combination of real world plus in-world', where a teacher delivers a face-to-face lesson and then arranges to meet his or her student for a follow-up class in a virtual world such as 'Second Life'. Furthermore, computer-assisted language learning in general has been described as 'context specific', and a number of local uses of the term 'BL' also exist within various educational settings, both national and institutional. For example, as some governments switch from course books to CD Rom or web-based material, the term has been applied to the blending (or combination) of print and digital materials.

There are also a number of 'dimensions' associated with definitions of BL, such as 'breadth' and 'connotation'. Thus, *Blended Learning* is the use of two or more distinct methods of training. This may include combinations such:

1. blending classroom instruction with on-line instruction
2. blending on-line instruction with access to a coach or faculty member
3. blending simulations with structured courses
4. blending on-the-job training with brown bag informal sessions
5. blending managerial coaching with e-learning activities

The Growth of Blended Learning

The blended approach to instruction has seen a steady increase in the past years, and survey data indicates that administrators in higher education expect that trend to continue. According to the Handbook of Blended Learning, a majority of respondents in a 2006 survey expect a dramatic rise in the use of blended learning as an instructional format, eventually encompassing 40% of course offerings within the next 6 years. Research from the University of Central Florida has indicated that faculty and student satisfaction with BL is high, and that the majority of both students and instructors would be willing to participate in future blended courses based on their past experiences with the format.

The Appeal of Blended Learning

Why has a blended approach been welcomed by faculty and students?

From a pedagogical perspective, blended learning's aim to join the best of classroom face-to-face learning experiences with the best of online learning experiences allows for:

1. An increase is learning outcome measures and lowering of attrition rates vs. fully online courses (Dziuban, Hartman & Moskal, 2004).

2. An opportunity for students to practice technology skills in navigating online course materials and possibility creating digital content for assignments.
3. An increase in student-instructor and student-student interaction through the use of course communication tools like discussion forums.
4. The ability to reserve face-to-face time for interactive activities, such as higher-level discussions, small group work, debates, demonstrations, or lab activities.

From a student perspective, the appeal of blended learning includes:

1. Flexibility of schedule: learn any-time, anywhere.
2. Control: students have some level of control over the pacing of their learning. Difficult concepts can be reviewed as often as necessary.
3. Convenience of an online class with many of the social aspects of a face-to-face class.

Format of Blended learning

When choosing to explore blended learning as a course format, there are several dimensions to course planning and development that should be considered:

Technology

Just like online courses, hybrid/blended courses are dependent on several technologies to function. These can include:

1. learning management systems
2. digital libraries

3. mobile technologies
4. streaming audio and/or video media
5. reusable learning objects and materials

Integration

Online materials are central to a blended course's success, and the students' work online must be relevant to the in-class activities. Aycock, Garnham, & Kaleta (2002) at the University of Wisconsin's blended learning effort revealed the importance of integration:

"The project's participants emphasized this point repeatedly. When asked, 'What would I do differently?' they were united in their response: 'I'd devote more attention to integrating what was going on in the classroom with the online work.' This was true even though the project's faculty development sessions repeatedly emphasized the importance of connecting in-class material with out-of-class assignments. One instructor responded emphatically, 'Integrate online with face-to-face, so there aren't two separate courses.' We found it impossible to stress integrating face-to-face and online learning too much."

Students can be critical of blended instruction if they felt the face-to-face and time-out-of-class components of the course were not well integrated.

Organization

For the most part, the blended format will be new to students, and they will benefit greatly from a clear rationale for its use. Instructors may need to explain the model and why it was chosen. A carefully constructed syllabus can provide much of the information about course structure for students; information like when and where the face-to-face meetings will be held, when and how assignments should be submitted, and what exactly will occur during the class meeting times are all critical aspects of the course that may not be obvious to those students new to blended learning.

Interaction

Research indicates that student satisfaction with the blended format is highly dependent on the level of interaction with instructors and other students. Instructors can address interaction issues by providing time during the face to face sessions for discussion, in addition to using available online discussion tools such as ANGEL discussion forums.

Student Expectations

Blended learning students require a greater ability to regulate their work and manage their own time. This is because they have fewer in-class meetings, and thus may not realize that they are falling behind in the course. Many blended instructors report significant problems with students not taking responsibility for their courses and with students' poor time management skills. In addition, some instructors have found that students occasionally assume that online and blended courses are inherently "easier" than traditional face-to-face courses. This can create problems when the rigors of the course surpass the expectations of some students. Again, a well-constructed syllabus can provide the essential details on what exactly is expected of students, thereby mitigating possible confusion on the part of students.

Role of instructor in blended learning

The instructor can combine two or more methods of teaching method. A typical example of blended learning methodology would be a combination of technology-based materials and face-to-face sessions to present content. An instructor can begin a course with a well-structured introductory lesson in the classroom, and then proceed with follow-up materials online. Blended learning can also be applied to the integration of e-learning with a Learning Management System using computers in a physical classroom, along with face-to-face instruction· Guidance is suggested early in the process, to be used more sparingly as learners gain expertise

The role of the instructor is critical as this requires a transformation process to that of learning facilitator. Quite often, with the increase of baby boomers going back to school and pursuing higher education the skills required for technology use are limited. Instructors then find themselves more in the role of assisting students with computer skills and applications, helping them access the internet, and encouraging them to be independent learners. Blended learning takes time for both the instructor and learner to adapt to this relatively new instructional concept.

Conclusion

Learning requires some sort of experience to take place. And the experience may be quite different for each learner in that we have to consider differences in (Banathy, 1968):

1. interest spans
2. needs
3. aptitudes
4. achievements
5. variations of time needed to master a specific learning task
6. abilities to deal with abstractness or concreteness
7. degree to which a learner needs to be guided
8. abilities to deal with complexities
9. abilities to manipulate objects (such as equipment or machines)

10.the degree to which imaginations can be involved

11.degrees to motivate creativity

12.problem solving differences

A systems approach to instruction implies a scientific study of the kind of instruction required by each learner, the time when it is needed, and the appropriate design, organization, and operation of a system which can achieve behavioral goals. In its broadest sense, an instructional system is a set of interrelated components (not aids or adjuncts) in mutual interaction. Thus, good instruction provides individual learning experiences within the learning environment by using a mixture of media, strategies, and methods. These learning experiences promote interactions that allow the learners to recall information so that it may be remembered and combine it with other experiences so that new knowledge bases may be formed.

References

1. Pellowe, Adams, Elliott, Murrell, and Cox, "The use of an blended learning infection prevention programme in the pre-registration nursing curriculum", Journal of Infection Prevention, v.11, UU, Pp.55 – 57, 2010.

2. Smeekens, Broekhuijsen-van Henten, Sitting, Russell, and Van de Putte., "Successful blended learning programme on the detection of child abuse in Emergency Departments: a randomised controlled trial", Arch. Dis. Child., 2011.

3. Zainab, "Book Review: Blended Learning: Tools for Teaching and Training by Barbara Allan 2007", Journal of Librarianship and Information Science, 2008.

20

Multimedia Programme in Perceiving Human Anatomy Among Students

Introduction

Research work is being continuously done in the field of science and also in the related teaching methods and materials. In order to keep pace with the development of science, the need for new instructional strategies was greatly felt. One such innovative teaching strategy, called multimedia programme, has been chosen and studied by the investigator in this research work. Upgrading Biology curriculum by introducing Human anatomy demands a change in the instructional strategy. The need for developing an instructional strategy for teaching Human anatomy and physiology is very important to make the teachers and students aware of the scientific principles that govern the advances being made in medicine. The functions of the internal organs of human body can be easily explained through a multimedia programme. This also saves the use of expensive chemicals and sophisticated instruments which are beyond the reach of higher secondary schools. In schools, the required equipment to explain the human anatomy is not available. In this situation, the working mechanism of internal organs can be explained by a multimedia programme, which when used as an instructional strategy will make the task of learning human anatomy easier, effective and less expensive. The present study aims to find out the effectiveness of multimedia programme in perceiving human anatomy among higher secondary students in Tindivanam.

A samples of 100 higher secondary students selected randomly were studied. A questionnaire method of survey was used to find out the effectiveness of multimedia programme in perceiving human anatomy. The data were collected by using questionnaire as an instrument. Primary data were collected by conducting direct structured interview using questionnaire. All the respondents were asked the same questions in the same fashion and they were informed the purpose of study. Mean, SD, and t-test analysis was applied to test the hypotheses. The findings and observations are the result and outcome of the interpretations made during the study of analysis. The result found that majority of the higher secondary students satisfied about multimedia programme.

In view of growing importance of science education, old concepts of science teaching have therefore, rather become completely outmoded and an entirely new ethos and approach to science curriculum have come into existence. Moreover, unprecedented development of scientific research, new discoveries, and new methods of investigation, in the early twentieth century, has created a need and urge to examine and reorganize science teaching programmes at all levels in schools. Institutions are functioning in an era of rapidly emerging new technologies. Some of them, like information and communications technology, have fuelled a veritable explosion of rising expectations everywhere. When such is the pace of developmental processes, it becomes fairly imperative on the part of the students not only to possess sound knowledge and understanding of fundamental concepts, but also to understand and appreciate the ramifications of various developments in the field of science and technology, especially in the context of their future career. The situation underscores the significance of research in science education and it is time for the educationists to evolve a proper and appropriate strategy for teaching science.

At the Higher Secondary level, the science subject is divided into Physics, Chemistry, Botany, and Zoology according to Tamil Nadu State Board syllabus. Zoology deals with the life history, distribution, structure, reproduction, and importance of animals including Homosapiens, the human beings. 'Human anatomy' is one of the units of the Zoology subject. Human anatomy is the branch of anatomy devoted to the structure of the human body. In general the study of human anatomy helps the students to do their higher studies in Medicine, Physiotherapy, Nursing, Degree courses like B.Sc., Zoology, and Microbiology etc. Apart from acquiring the technical knowledge, it is necessary for human beings to know and control their own systems of their body for healthy life. Hence the investigator has selected the unit "human anatomy" to teach through multimedia programme for the higher secondary students in the present investigation.

An instructional or teaching strategy refers to a pattern of teaching act that serves to attain certain goals and to guard against others. An instructional strategy is a purposefully-conceived and determined plan of action. It also occupies a central position in formal education. Instructional strategies aim at establishing relationship between teaching inputs and learning outputs, mainly in terms of realizing the learning outcomes. Instructional strategies include teaching methods, approaches and techniques.

Methods of instruction may be teacher-centered such as Historical method, Biographical method, Lecture method, Lecture-demonstration method or pupil-centered method which includes group methods such as project method, discussion, seminar and workshop. The pupil-centered methods also include individual methods such as programmed instruction, Computer Aided Instruction, Instructional Modules and Multimedia packages.

Review of Literature

Chang, Kuo-En et al. (2008) studied the effects of learning support in simulation-based physics learning. The results of the study revealed that the outcome for learning about the basic characteristics of an optical lens was significantly better for simulation-based learning than for laboratory learning.

Djeassilane (2008) investigated the effect of computer aided instruction (CAI) in enhancing the academic achievement of higher secondary students in commerce. The findings of the study showed that the computer aided instruction was effective in helping the students of the experimental group to perform better in the post-test. It proved the effectiveness of the computer aided instruction in commerce developed by the investigator. And also it was found that the experimental students had more favourable attitude towards computer assisted instruction.

Garnett, Hackling and Oliver (2009) developed an interactive multimedia package to improve students' understanding of the particulate basis of chemical reaction, and their ability to interpret chemical equations and solve problems based on equations. The study showed that Interactive multimedia provided learners with access to a rich information source and appropriate activities to promote learning and understanding.

Junaidu, Sahalu (2009) studied effectiveness of multimedia in learning & teaching data structures online. This paper explores and reports on the importance of creating multimedia-rich course content and the important role that animations can play in creating a successful online learning experience. Results indicated that students consistently perform much better in questions requiring application of material taught in carefully animated algorithms. These results should carry over to other educational environments.

Liao, Yuen-kuang C., Chang, Huei-wen and Chen, Yu-wen (2009) compared the effects of computer applications (i.e., computer-assisted instruction, computer simulations, and Web-based learning) versus traditional instruction on elementary school students' achievement in Taiwan. The results suggest that computer application instruction is more effective than traditional instruction for elementary school students in Taiwan.

O'Day, Danton (2010) studied on "using animations to teach biology: past & future research on the attributes that underlie pedagogically sound animations". Multiple technical resources (commonly referred to as multimedia) are currently used by many instructors to communicate difficult topics and concepts to their students in meaningful ways. Various sources have shown that animations are more effective than static sequential images. This study evaluated how animations can be and have been used as effective teaching and learning tools in biology and what more needs to be done to understand their true value.

Ozmen, Haluk (2010) studied on "The influence of CAI on students' conceptual understanding of chemical Bonding and attitude towards chemistry: A case for Turkey". The results of this study suggested that teaching-learning of topics in chemistry related to chemical bonding can be improved by the use of computer-assisted teaching materials.

Ponraj and Nellaiyapen (2010) investigated the effectiveness of CAI in teaching Zoology. The major finding of the study showed that the experimental group performed better than the Control group in the post-test. The results of the study revealed that experimental method of teaching is more effective than the traditional method of teaching the topic 'Nucleus' in Zoology.

Pryor, Caroline and Bitter, Gary (2010) used multimedia to teach in-service teachers and studied its impacts on learning, application, and retention. The study found that the video modeling in the module was effective in helping teachers learn, and discourse strategies were learned, applied, and retained.

Rotbain, Marbach-Ad and Stavy (2011) used a computer animation to teach high school molecular biology. The achievements of the experimental group were compared with those of a control group. Analysis of the post-test showed that the mean score of the experimental group was significantly higher than the mean score of the control group.

Venkataraman (2011) prepared software packages (CAI) for XI standard physics and studied the effectiveness of its among selected modes of CAI in physics in relation to learners' personality. The results of the study showed that the CAI is effective with different modes. Computer Assisted Instruction shows significant difference in the achievement of different instructional objectives. Further Computer Assisted Instruction enhances the retention of the learnt content.

Vernadakis et al. (2012) examined the effect of multimedia computer-assisted instruction (MCAI), traditional instruction (TI), and combined instruction (CI) methods on learning the skill of shooting in basketball. Additionally, a comparison of the students' attitudes towards the MCAI and TI methods was made. Students took pre-, post-, and retention written test covering techniques and rules of the games. Post-test results indicated no significant differences between the groups concerning the written test. Nevertheless, the attitude test scores of the CI group were more favourable to MCAI method than the TI method. Retention test results showed that groups retained the knowledge acquisition. However, the combined method of instruction tended to be the most effective for cognitive learning.

Victor, Adeosun Olufemi (2012) investigated the relative effects of three multi-media instructional packages on Nigerian students' achievement in social studies. The purpose was to determine which of the combinations of videotape recording presentation, pictures and the chalk and talk method; the combination of audiotape recording presentation, pictures and the chalk and talk method and the combination of pictures and the chalk and talk method. The study revealed that the combination of pictures and the chalk and talk method was most effective among the packages tested in the learning of social studies.

Objectives

1. To develop a Multimedia Programme for the unit of Human anatomy from XI standard Zoology subject in order to teach the higher secondary students.
2. To find out the effectiveness of Multimedia Programme in teaching Human anatomy among higher secondary students.

Methodology

The methodology adopted for the study is explained in detail. The sampling technique, size of the sample, variables of the study, description of the tool used and administration of tool are elaborated.

Sample

A samples of 100 higher secondary students in selected randomly were studied in Tindivanam Town.

Data Collection

The present study aims at developing and using Multimedia programme for perceiving human anatomy for higher secondary students to enable them to understand the concepts very easily through individualized instructional technique. It is maintained that the Multimedia programme may reduce monotony in the classroom by bringing out real life situations and motivate them for self-study and provides opportunities for individual pace and ability.

The study intends to develop a multimedia programme for human anatomy for XI standard Zoology subject prescribed by Tamil Nadu State Board Syllabus and find out the effectiveness of the Multimedia programme through experimentation in perceiving human anatomy among the higher secondary students. The study provides scope for the development and use of many Multimedia programmes in the concerned discipline as well as other disciplines for the benefit of learners of different categories. Hence the multimedia programme can be used as an individualized instructional technique for the students of different categories in the science subjects as well as other subjects.

Analysis and Interpretation

Performance of control group students between the pre test and post test in human anatomy.

The Mean, Standard Deviation and Co-efficient of Variation were computed for the control group students in their performance in human anatomy between the pre test and post test.

Table 1 : Distribution of Mean, Standard Deviation and Co-efficient of Variation on the performance of control group students between the pre test and post test in human anatomy

Group	N	Mean	S.D	CV
Pre test	100	42.69	13.60	31.86
Post test	100	52.46	13.28	25.31

The Co-efficient of Variation of the pre test and post test for the control group students was found to be 31.86 and 25.31, which reveals that the control group students are more consistent in their performance in human anatomy in the post test than the pre test. It reveals that the control group students have improved in their performance in human anatomy in the post test than the pre test.

To find out the significance of the difference between the control and experimental group students in their performance in human anatomy in the pre test, the 't' test was used.

Table 2 : Distribution of 't' value between the control and experimental group students in their performance in human anatomy in the pre test

Group	N	Mean	S.D	't' value	Level of Significant
Control	100	42.69	13.60	0.17	p>0.05
Experimental	100	43.31	12.59		

There is no significant difference between the control and experimental group students in their performance in human anatomy in the pre test.

The obtained 't' value 0.17 is not statistically significant since it is less than the table 't' value 1.96 for 50 df at 0.05 level of significance. Hence the null hypothesis is accepted. It shows that there is no significant difference between the control and experimental group students in their performance in human anatomy in the pre test. It is therefore concluded that both control and experimental group students have the same level of performance in human anatomy in the pre test.

To find out the significance of the difference between the control and experimental group students in their performance in human anatomy in the post test, the 't' test was used.

Table 3 : Distribution of 't' value between the control and experimental group students in their performance in human anatomy in the post test

Group	N	Mean	S.D	't' value	Level of Significant
Control	100	52.46	13.28	14.38	$p<0.05$
Experimental	100	92.81	5.31		

There is no significant difference between the control and experimental group students in their performance in human anatomy in the post test.

The obtained 't' value 14.38 is statistically significant since it is greater than the table 't' value 1.96 for 50 df at 0.05 level of significance. Hence the null hypothesis is rejected. It shows that there is significant difference between the control and experimental group students in their performance in human anatomy in the post test. It is therefore concluded that the experimental group students performed significantly better in human anatomy than that of control group students in the post test.

To find out the significance of the difference between the pre and post test mean scores of control group students in the performance in human anatomy, the 't' was used.

Table 4 : Distribution of 't' value for the pre and post test mean scores of control group students in the performance in human anatomy

Group	N	Mean	S.D	't' value	Level of Significant
Pre test	100	42.69	13.60	2.62	$p<0.05$
Post test	100	52.46	13.28		

There is no significant difference between the pre and post test mean scores of control group students in the performance in human anatomy.

The obtained 't' value 2.62 is statistically significant since it is greater than the table 't' value 1.96 for 50 df at 0.05 level of significance. Hence the null hypothesis is rejected. It shows that there is significant difference between the pre and post test mean scores of control group students in the performance in human anatomy. It is therefore concluded that the control group students have improved in their performance in human anatomy in the post test.

Suggestions

The present study aims at developing and using Multimedia programme for perceiving human anatomy for higher secondary students to enable them to understand the concepts very easily through individualized instructional technique. It is maintained that the Multimedia programme may reduce monotony in the classroom by bringing out real life situations and motivate them for self-study and provides opportunities for individual pace and ability.

Conclusion

The study intends to develop a multimedia programme for human anatomy for XI standard Zoology subject prescribed by Tamil Nadu State Board Syllabus and find out the effectiveness of the Multimedia programme through experimentation in perceiving human anatomy among the higher secondary students. The study provides scope for the development and use of many Multimedia programmes in the concerned discipline as well as other disciplines for the benefit of learners of different categories. Hence the multimedia programme can be used as an individualized instructional technique for the students of different categories in the science subjects as well as other subjects.

The present study reveals that the experiment group students who used multimedia programme performed significantly better than that of the control group students who did not use, which implies that the multimedia programme has tremendous impact upon the performance in human anatomy than the students learning through traditional method. This proves the effectiveness of the multimedia programme in human anatomy developed by the investigator.

The present study reveals that the performance of the control and experimental group students in the post test is significantly higher than the pre test. But the performance of the experimental group students in the post test is more significantly higher than the post test performance of control group students. Thus, it proves the supremacy of the multimedia programme over traditional method.

References

1. Chang, Kuo-En; Chen, Yu-Lung; Lin, He-Yan; Sung, Yao-Ting (2008). Effects of learning support in simulation-based physics learning. Computers & Education, 51(4): 1486-1498..

2. Djeassilane, N. (2008). Effect of computer aided instruction (CAI) in enhancing the academic achievement of higher secondary students in commerce. Unpublished Doctoral Dissertation, Alagappa University, Karaikudi.

3. Garnett, P., Hackling, M., & Oliver, R. (2009). Designing interactive multimedia materials to support concept development in beginning chemistry classes.

4. Junaidu, Sahalu (2009). Effectiveness of multimedia in learning & teaching data structures online. Turkish Online

Journal of Distance Education-TOJDE, 9(4), Article 7. Retrieved March.

5. Liao, Yuen-kuang C., Chang, Huei-wen & Chen, Yu-wen (2009). Effects of Computer Applications on Elementary School Students' Achievement: A Meta-Analysis of Students in Taiwan. Computers in the Schools, 24(3-4): 43-64. Retrieved.

6. O'Day, Danton H. (2010). Using animations to teach biology: past & future research on the attributes that underlie pedagogically sound animations. The American Biology Teacher, 70(5):274-278. Retrieved March 20.

7. Ozmen, Haluk (2010). The influence of Computer-Assisted Instruction on students' conceptual understanding of chemical Bonding and Attitude toward chemistry: A case for Turkey. Computers and Education, 51(1): 423-438. Retrieved March.

8. Ponraj, P., & Nellaiyapen, N. O. (2010). CAI in teaching Zoology. Research and Reflections on Education, 6(2): 18-21.

9. Pryor, Caroline R., & Bitter, Gary G. (2010). Using multimedia to teach in-service teachers: Impacts on learning, application, and retention. Computers in Human Behavior, 24 (6): 2668-2681. Retrieved March.

10. Rotbain, Y., Marbach-Ad, G., & Stavy, R. (2011). Using a computer animation to teach high school molecular biology. Journal of Science Education and Technology, 17(1): 49 – 58. Retrieved March.

11. Venkataraman, S. (2011). Relative effectiveness among selected modes of CAI in physics in relation to learner's personality. Unpublished Doctoral Dissertation, Annamalai University. Chidambaram.

12. Vernadakis, N., Zetou, E., Tsitskari, E., Giannousi, M., & Kioumourtzoglou, E. (2012). Student attitude and learning outcomes of multimedia computer-assisted versus traditional instruction in basketball. Education and Information Technologies, 13(3): 167-183.

13. Victor, Adeosun Olufemi (2012). Relative effects of three Multi-Media Instructional Packages on Nigerian student's achievement in Social Studies. Pakistan Journal of Social Sciences, 5 (5): 415 – 420. Retrieved March.

21

Role of ICT in Education

Introduction

In the modern era the role of ICT ,especially internet in the education sector plays an important role ,especially in the process of employing the technology into the educational activities. Education sector can be the most effective sector to anticipate and eliminate the negative impact of ICT .Internet technology can be the most effective way to increase the student's knowledge . In course of industrial , scientific and technological development, ICT has become an inevitable means of pedagogy in education.

Different Types of ICTs Their and in Education

1. Radio and television have been used widely as educational tools since 1920s and 1950s, respectively. There are three genera approaches to the use of radio and TV broadcasting in education; direct class room teaching, where broadcast programming substitutes for teachers on a temporary basis; school broadcasting ,where broadcasting programming

provides complementary teaching and learning resources otherwise not available and general educational programming over community ,national and international; stations , which provide general and informal educational opportunities.

2. Teleconferencing enables one to “interactive elect4ronic communication among people located at two or more different places”. There are four types of teleconferencing based on the nature and extent of interactivity and the sophistication of the technology (i) audio conferencing (ii) audio-graphic conferencing (iii) video conferencing and (iv) Web-based conferencing.

3. There are general approaches to the instructional use of computers and the internet ,namely learning about computers and the internet in ,which technological literacy is the end goal; Learning with the help of computers and the internet in which the technology facilitates learning across the curriculum and learning through computers and the internet ,integrating technological development skills with curriculum applications.

4. Learining with the technology means focusing on how the technology can be the means to learning and across the curriculum.

5. Many higher educational institutions offering distance education courses have started to leverage the internet to optimize quality of their programmes.

6. ICT gives students the opportunity to collaborate with scientists in conducting earth science research. Participating students periodically take measurements of the atmosphere, water, soils and land around their schools. It also provides teachers with guidelines and materials for structured learning activities that take off from the students hands-on experience.

7. ICT provides e-journals ,which cover all aspects of information and communication technology theories and applications.
8. People learn with ICT and digital media as an integrated aspect of everyday course of living whether in school at home or at work.
9. ICT provides Blended Learning which refers to an educational experience created cost-effectively using a mix of integrated distance learning technologies such as video conferencing ,e-learning, videos and CD-ROM

Advantages of the Use of ICT in Education

ICT encompasses all those gadgets that deal with the processing of information for better and effective communication. In education, communication process takes place between teachers, students, management and administrative personnel which requires plenty of data to be stored for retrieval as and when required, to be disseminated or transmitted in the desired format. The hardware and software like OHP, Television, Radio, Computers and related software are used in the educational process. However ICT today is mostly focused on the use of Computer technology for processing the data. In this context, advantages of ICT in education can be listed down as follows:

Quick access to information

Information can be accessed in seconds by connecting to the internet and surfing through Web pages.

Easy availability of updated data:

Sitting at home or at any comfortable place the desired information can be accessed easily. This helps the students to learn the updated content. Teachers too can keep themselves abreast of the latest teaching learning strategies and related technologies.

Connecting Geographically dispersed regions:

With the advancement of ICT, education does not remain restricted within four walls of the educational institutions. Students from different parts of the world can learn together by using online, offline resources. This would result in the enriching learning experience. Such collaborative learning can result in developing.

Facilitation of learning

ICT has contributed in shifting the focus on learning than teaching. ICT helps students to explore knowledge to learn the content through self study. Teacher can help the students by ensuring the right direction towards effective learning. Situational learning, Programmed learning, many Online learning courses are some of the example of self learning strategies that are being utilized with the help of ICT.

Catering to the Individual differences

ICT can contribute in catering to individual needs of the students as per their capabilities and interest. Crowded class rooms have always been a challenge for the teacher to consider the needs of every student in the class.

Wider range of communication media

With the advent of ICT, different means of communication are being introduced in the teaching learning process. Offline learning, on line learning, blended learning is some of the resources that can be used in educational institutions. Collaborative learning, individualized learning strategies can enhance the quality of group as well as individual learning.

Facilitation of learning

ICT has contributed in shifting the focus on learning than teaching. ICT helps students to explore knowledge to learn the content through self study. Teacher can help the students by ensuring the right direction towards effective learning. Situational learning, Programmed learning, many Online learning courses are some of the example of self learning strategies that are being utilized with the help of ICT.

Catering to the Individual differences:

ICT can contribute in catering to individual needs of the students as per their capabilities and interest. Crowded class rooms have always been a challenge for the teacher to consider the needs of every student in the class.

Wider learning opportunities for pupils

Application of latest ICT in education has provided many options to the learners to opt for the course of their choices. Many Online courses are available for them to select any as per their aptitude and interest. Students can evaluate their own progress through different quizzes, ready to use online tests. This can ensure fulfillment of the employment required in the job market thus minimizing the problem of unemployment. It can also provide more efficient and effective citizens to the society as per the changing needs.

Conclusion

To summarize, when using ICTs in your adult learning work, make sure and

1. ICT and e-learning offers opportunity to raise educational standards in schools

2. Large range of ICT tools are available for teaching and learning
3. Closes the gap of "Digital Divide"
4. Involvement of teachers and parents is important
5. Schools will need funding, access and training
6. Mix, supplement with different media
7. Mix and experiment with formats and treatments
8. Greater emphasis upon substance, less on style
9. Use of graphics, animation
10. Summarizing and recap of main points
11. Build in interactivity

References

1. Digital Media and Learning. The John D. and Catherine T. MacArthur Foundation
2. Digital Learning (India) December 2011
3. Victoria L.Tinio,'ICT in Education Sector', Inside Magazine
4. Society for ICT 2002.Basic Principles.

22

Effective Blended Learning Practice

Introduction

Blended learning practices are becoming the basis for much of today's academic teaching, research collaborative writing, course design and professional learning. Though the term blended learning is becoming widespread in use and is often used to describe student learning through traditional face-to-face teaching integrating some online teaching, its application to all academic and professional practice extends the term blended learning practices and requires a more complex definition

The term blended learning was defined and the rationale for the symposium discussed. The complexity of blended learning and its features and the issues involved in its integration into teaching and learning was introduced and overviewed in relation to the topics covered in the book. The introductory overview raised key questions that were then discussed by panel presenters'.

Teaching and Learning Strategies

Online discussions offer a different discussion medium from face-to-face discussions and creating an effective Pedagogy which engages campus-based students is a challenge. This research investigated campus-based student perspective about online discussions using a case study approach. It highlighted the need for complementarily of online and face-to-face media and the need for explicit integration in the course, and especially in the classroom. Key influential features arising from the CMC medium and the Learning design are presented and recommendations for practice are provided redesigned to take advantage of the affordances' offered by a blended learning approach. The resign process described here drew on three areas – the research and practice base of adult learning, knowledge of and experience.

Teacher Transitions and Professional Learning

Blended learning represents a significant departure from either face to face or fully online learning experiences" (Garrison & Kanuka 2004). The current trend towards blended learning is fuelled by a combination of pedagogical, practical and strategic factors, Professional development must therefore interact with a complex combination of separate, yet interdependent factors. An approach pursued at one institution used design-based research and an accredited tertiary teaching program, thus acknowledging the context specific nature of best practices. What other ways can university teachers are empowered to develop an effective blend of face to face and online activity?

Systematic adoption of blended learning practices is complex as it depends on a series of contextual factors. Institutional environments have their unique social and political contexts and their own policy frameworks, technology, work practices, training programs, funding grants and faculty structures. Understanding the power and polities that inter relate these assists with the understanding of introducing blended learning approaches to the institution. An institution-wide qualitative research study conducted in a large multi-campus Australian university forms the basis of this study which found that the technology impacts on the institution and its practices, and in turn the institutional context shapes the adoption and use of technology. The study showed that introducing blended-learning is disruptive, imposing challenges at all levels across the institution. The presentation will review these challenges and discuss its impact on teaching staff.

Socialization

Students are more successful working together when they know each other (Aycock, Garnham & Kaleta,2002) and the socialization process progresses faster in a face-to-face environment. Therefore, use the first face – to face classroom meeting to start student socialization.

Tips For Succsess

Give students tips on how to succeed in your course. For example, log-in to your course at a minimum three times per week.

Assessment

Provide regular opportunities for students to demonstrate their knowledge and proficiency with the course content.

Feedback

Provide regular and timely feedback to students and, when appropriate, give them opportunities to correct their work.

Technology Instructions

Hopefully, your institution has instructions on how to use

the tools in your course management system (CMS) and you can point your students to these instructions. If not, you need to write clear instructions for the tools used in your course. Also, you need instructions for common issues encountered by students such as resetting passwords.

Communication Policies or Protocols

Provide your communication policies for classroom and online. Your policies should include methods of communication such as e-mail for personal communication. To avoid answering the same question for every student, use public communication tools such as discussions to communicate with the entire class. You might have a discussion topic to post questions to the professor. Be sure to address "tone" in electronic communications and netiquette. IF grammar and spelling are important make sure to conclude them in your policies.

Time Management

Your students may need help with time management skills. Younger students tend to have difficulty managing their time and keeping up with assignments. On the other hand, adult learners are often overcommitted between family and job responsibilities. Here are a few tips to help with time management:

1. Log your daily activities for a week so your discussions in time management are grounded in experience (Aycock, Graham & Kaleta, 2002).
2. Provide a printer=friendly schedule with all assignments and due dates.
3. Use announcements, calendars, or periodic messages as reminders of due dates.
4. Use adaptive releases connect to keep students on track.

5. For graduate courses, consider opening all the content and allowing students to work ahead. For assignments like discussions, students may post their initial comment in advance but need to return to the discussion when the rest of the class is present.

Academic Resources

Academic resources on your campus such as the writing center, library, bookstore, computer store, and student support services, etc.

Technical Resources

Provide links to your institutions help desk, tutorials, instructions, frequently asked question, etc.

Conclusion

Blended courses which are also known as mixed mode of courses become popular at present. The traditional face-to-face instruction and the old classroom teaching are being slowly replaced by online learning. At present part of the causes is imparted by web based instruction. When it is found more useful blended courses can be fully replaced.

References

1. Aycock, A., Garnham, C., & Kaleta, R. (March 20, 2002). Lessons learned from the hybrid course project. *Teaching with Technology Today*, 8(6), 1-6.
2. Simmons College Checklists, http://at.simmons.edu/blendedlearning/implement/simmons.php
3. Gerbic, P. (2009). Including online discussions within campus-based students' learning environments. In E.

Stacey & P. Gerbic (Eds.), *Effective blended learning practices: Evidenced-based perspectives in ICT-Facilitated Education* (pp. 21-38). Hershey, PA: Information Science Reference.

4. Gerbic, P., & Stacey, E. (2009). Conclusion. In E. Stacey & P. Gerbic (Eds.), *Effective blended learning practices: Evidenced-based perspectives in ICT-facilitated education* (pp. 298-311). Hershey, PA:
5. Gunn, C., & Blake, A. (2009). Blending technology into an academic practice qualification for university teachers. In A. Stacey & P. Gerbic (Eds.), *Effective blended learning practices. Evidence-based perspectives in ICT-facilitated education,* (pp. 259-279). Hershey, PA: Information Science
6. Mackey, J. (2009). Virtual learning and real communities: Online professional development for teachers.
7. In E. Stacey & P. Gerbic (Eds.), *Effective blended learning practices. Evidence-based perspectives in ICT-facilitated education,* . Hershey, PA: Information Science Reference.

23

Blended Learning

Introduction

Blended Learning refers to a mixing of different learning environments. The phrase has many specific meanings based upon the context in which it is used. Blended learning gives learners and teachers a potential environment to learn and teach more effectively. Blended learning increases the options for greater quality and quantity of human interaction in a learning environment. Blended learning offers learners the opportunity to be both together and apart. A community of learners can interact at anytime and anywhere because of the benefits that computer-mediated educational tools provide. Blended learning provides a good mix of technologies and interactions, resulting in a socially supported, constructive, learning experience, this is especially significant given the profound effect that it could have on distance learning. A typical example of blended learning methodology would be a combination of technology-based materials and face-to-face sessions to present content. Blended learning can also be applied to the integration of e-learning with a Learning Management System using computers in a physical classroom, along with face-to-face instruction. Guidance is suggested early in the process, to be used more sparingly as learners gain expertise. Learning and Development people have accepted that the learning landscape needs to include a wide range of learning methods, and are having varying degrees of success in using blended learning to its full potential. Blended learning is well-established but not necessarily well blended. Blended learning solutions are an important part of the learning & development landscape and traditional learning methods frequently or sometimes. Combining more than one learning method into a solution is no longer unusual. Our respondents did, however, highlight the dangers of having a team of designers working in their silos on each different learning element, rather than there being a single vision for the blend to which each learning method contributes.

History of Blended Learning

Technology-based training emerged as an alternative to instructor-led training in the 1960s on mainframes and mini-computers. The major advantage that blended learning offers is scale, whereas one instructor can only teach so many people. One example is Programmed Logic for Automatic Teaching Operations, a system developed by the University of Illinois and Control Data. Programmed Logic for Automatic Teaching Operations in particular had a long history of innovations and offered coursework from elementary to the college level.

Advantages

Proponents of blended learning argue that by incorporating the asynchronous Internet communication technology into courses serves to facilitate a simultaneous independent and collaborative learning experience and this incorporation is a major contributor to student satisfaction and success in such courses. The use of information and communication technologies has been found to improve access to as well as student attitudes towards learning. By incorporating information technology into class projects, communication between lecturers and part-time students was improved, and students were able to better evaluate their understanding of course material via the use of "computer-based qualitative and quantitative assessment modules" in a study by Alexander and McKenzie (1998).

Disadvantages

Blended learning has a strong dependence on the technical resources with which the blended learning experience is delivered these tools need to be reliable, easy to use, and up to date in order for the use of the Internet to have a meaningful impact on the learning experience. Additionally, IT literacy can serve as a significant barrier for students attempting to get access to the course materials, making the availability of high quality technical support paramount. It has been observed that the use of lecture recording technologies can result in students falling behind on the material in a study performed across four different universities, it was found that only half of the students watched the lecture videos on a regular basis, and nearly 40% of students watched several weeks worth of videos in one sitting.

The definition of blended learning is a formal education program in which a student learns:

1. at least in part through online learning, with some element of student control over time, place, path, and/or pace;
2. at least in part in a supervised brick-and-mortar location away from home;
3. the modalities along each student's learning path within a course or subject are connected to provide an integrated learning experience.

Models of Blended Learning

1. The **Rotation Model** includes four sub-models:

a) Station Rotation
b) Lab Rotation
c) Flipped Classroom
d) Individual Rotation.

Rotation Model: A course or subject in which students rotate on a ûxed schedule or at the teacher's discretion between learning modalities, at least one of which is online learning. Other modalities might include activities such as small-group or full-class instruction, group projects, individual tutoring, and pencil-and-paper assignments.

Station Rotation: A course or subject in which students experience the Rotation model within a contained classroom or group of classrooms. The Station Rotation model differs from the Individual Rotation model because students rotate through all of the stations, not only those on their custom schedules.

Lab Rotation: A course or subject in which students rotate to a computer lab for the online-learning station.

Flipped Classroom: A course or subject in which students participate in online learning off-site in place of traditional homework .The primary delivery of content and instruction is online, which differentiates a Flipped Classroom from students who are merely doing homework practice online at night. Individual Rotation: A course or subject in which each student has an individualized playlist and does not necessarily rotate to each available station or modality. An algorithm or teachers sets individual student schedules.

2. Flex Model

A course or subject in which online learning is the backbone of student learning, even if it directs students to oûine activities at times. Students move on an individually customized, ûuid schedule among learning modalities. The teacher of record is on-site, and students learn mostly on the brick-and-mortar campus, except for any homework assignments.

3. Enriched Virtual Model

A course or subject in which students have required face-to-face learning sessions with their teacher of record and then are free to complete their remaining coursework remote from the face-to-face teacher. Many Enriched Virtual programs began as full-time online schools and then developed blended programs to provide students with brick-and-mortar school experiences. The Enriched Virtual model differs from the Flipped Classroom because in Enriched Virtual programs, students meet face-to-face with their teachers every weekday

Blended Learning can support a variety of informal learning processes. This performance support function is an increasingly important part of the job for many corporate training departments. Blended Learning expands the traditional role of training beyond its usual scope of formal training by providing a robust set of tools that allow employees to obtain the information and instruction they independently and uniquely need, all within the daily flow of work. Blended Learning captures the best of both worlds by allowing learners to pick and choose how they want to learn and offers them greater flexibility and convenience about when they want to learn.

Blended Learning offers a variety of formal and informal learning assets to utilize within e-learning. Apart from the well-used instructor-led training, other formal learning options include virtual classroom training, games, simulations, testing and evaluation. Informal learning assets include online books and articles, videos, podcasts, learning and knowledge portals, social networks, wikis, blogs and forums, and much more. One significant benefit of taking the blended approach is that we start to think of learning as more of a process than an event or series of events. Because it has so many modalities available, it can touch colleagues with a variety of learning opportunities, most of which occur or reside outside the traditional classroom. Retention of knowledge and application of learning – and therefore lasting behavior change – can really be multiplied as a result. It increases staff engagement as they realize that development is happening all the time and it also increases involvement of supervisors and managers in the development of their staff. Successful adoption of a blended learning approach to enhance the effectiveness and efficiency of teaching and learning will require the following:

1. Creation of clear institutional direction and policy
2. Frame the potential, increase awareness, and commit
3. Establishment of a single point of support, quality assurance and project management
4. Creation of an innovation fund to provide the financial support and incentives to faculty and departments to initiate blended learning course transformations
5. Investment in establishing a reliable and accessible, technology infrastructure
6. Strategic selection of prototype projects that prove to be exceptionally successful exemplars of effective learning
7. Development of formal instructional design support available through a blended format
8. Systematic evaluation of satisfaction and success of the teaching, learning, technology and administration of new course
9. Create a task group to address issues, challenges and opportunities as well as communicate and recommend new directions to the University community.

Conclusions

It is inevitable that campus-based higher education institutions will adopt blended learning approaches in a significant way. As has been demonstrated by several institutions, once there is clear policy and strong leadership, the evolution will be quick. In a matter of a few short years, higher education institutions can be transformed in a manner consistent with their values and mitigating the fiscal and pedagogical challenges and deficiencies currently challenging the quality of the classroom experience. The academic benefit, evidence, and competitive advantages are clear; only the will and commitment remains. Blended learning can begin the necessary process of redefining higher education institutions as being learning centered and facilitating a higher learning experience. we explore the use of blended learning, it is important that we assess and evaluate its effectiveness. Tracking transformations resulting from the use of blended learning approaches, with respect to learning outcomes, student satisfaction, retention and achievement, are important to use as baseline measures of change that result from blended learning courses. In addition to assessing the learning outcomes, the learning process should also be assessed. Assessing and evaluating the effects of blended learning on the learning process in terms of higher levels of learning, critical and reflective thinking is a priority. It is essential that researchers begin to explore the impact of blended learning in achieving more meaningful learning experiences.

24

Digi-class For Tomorrow

Introduction

One can achieve victory through many factors but education is something which gives endless victory and satisfaction. But to achieve it (education), the path followed should be very systematic and diplomatic. For a country to develop, it should have people who are determined to take quality education. This is very true and we believe in this since many decades. But the education system that we had around four to five decades before is not same as today's education. Many changes are evident from the input as well as the output that is got from the present generation. Earlier it used to be very monotonous where teacher centered education was followed and the students had very less possibilities and opportunities to express their views and creative talents. It was only to teach but nothing was tested at the level of application. To be very precise no ground work was done on this. Strategy of applying the skill learnt for the sake of problem solving was not known to the then generation. Major change was experienced only when child centered education was introduced and learner was considered as the major part of teaching learning programme. In fact, teacher also plays a major role as a guide. But teacher role is very much to bring out the hidden talents in the students.

Why is digital technology essential in education?

The means to fulfill the present requirement is by including technology in present education. This has been started and the process of universalizing is into action. It is not just using computers during teaching or learning but also to bring innovation by using this computer technology. Information and communication technology is something which is already in picture. ICT tries to pick up every kind of student and present education. This is one of the best of many modern techniques as it overcomes the difficulties faced by the conventional classroom teacher due to individual differences. But again the preparation of programmes for different groups of students based on their ability is a task for the teachers.

Today's education is not same as yesterdays. Similarly today's will not be the same as tomorrow's education. There is a need for updating of modern skill time to time. Young people of today should be prepared for emerging digital society of tomorrow. More emphasize on the need for the education system to embrace technology and foster digital literacy at an early stage to create next generation of informed and responsible participants.

Educating a digital society is the way forward. Actual teacher should have sound knowledge about the latest technology. The present generations that are in need of education are way ahead in terms of ability to use digital technology. Teacher should be very enthusiastic in acquiring new digital skills. This would be one way to help all groups of students. Slow learners would be category of students who will be very much favored by this technique of using digital technology during teaching. Proper and effective adaptation of these digital skills would help both students as well as children.

Following are the major aspects to be kept in mind while preparing materials using digital technology.

1. Involvement of both course creator and the teacher. Here course creator means one who builds the syllabus. It should be combined effort of both of them during whole stages of course building implementation.

2. Arranging the content in educationally sound sequence Arranging in Simple to complex or concrete to abstract manner, as this is for all category of students.

3. Content analysis Breaking the existing content into manageable units for the learner. Every unit should accomplish specific objectives. This helps the learners to have easy access over the content.

4. Teacher can standardize the content by making a common course framework by making flowcharts/course maps. This should be done only after the thorough analysis of content, setting the goals to be achieved after the completion, structure and size of lesson.

5. Adapting to the technique of presenting the content with the help of PowerPoint presentations would help to some extent but not for all the units.

6. Use of audio/ video presentation of the lesson, which would make learning

7. Making of interactive exercises and different brain storming activities, other than theoretical content. These activities ensure the involvement of children.

8. Providing the learning material in a language level that is easy and appropriate for the learner community. Use of shortcuts, acronyms etc would be helpful for slow learners.

9. Making content on the screen in such a way that it would be easy for the learners to scroll and learn without difficulty.

10. The teacher should decide as of how the students would navigate, when the content is presented. And this should not be a barrier for later on assessment.

11. The material can be presented to the students either in printed form or can be downloaded.

Training is regarded as key to success, as long as digital education is concerned. If this digital technology is to be applied in full fledged manner among the present generation, teacher should be taught about the use of this technology in fruitful way. For getting maximum benefits from digital learning, the cost for it is extending facilities for the teachers to standardize the digital content using modern technology. Providing proper training for teachers to do this with confidence and motivation is very essential. It is to be remembered that teachers remain central to the learning process as they should plan, prepare, assess and provide follow up activities to the children. Mere use of technology in class rooms would not change the teaching learning process. It is a technique that is for enabling the teachers to transform their teaching practices and thereby impacts on student's achievement.

Merits of Using Digital Technology

1. It improves teacher's confidence and motivates them to learn new technology.

2. It enables the teacher to bring in required changes in teaching process.

3. It ensures effective participation of teacher in teaching learning process.

4. It widens the subject knowledge among teachers as they have to thoroughly analyze the content before presentation.

5. Narrow thinking and conventional method of teaching can be now forgotten as this digital age is all about broadening the horizon of knowledge using skill and creativity.
6. Teacher can create more of learner centric environment.
7. This method keeps the teachers updated.
8. It provides exposure to mixed effectiveness for the students because even difficult/abstract concept could be put across the students using pictures, PowerPoint presentations, simulations etc.

Demerits of Adapting Digital Technology in Present Day Education

1. It is difficult to provide training to all the teachers, as it requires wide coverage.
2. Government should take initiative of providing no cost training to all the teachers.
3. Every school should have the minimum facility of providing digital classes to the students, which is usually less in government run schools and rural background schools.
4. Teachers sometimes show negative attitude towards learning new concepts of digital technology.
5. Certain teachers feel shy to use this modern technology in public, and some are totally unaware of system/computer usage.
6. There is need of continuous updating of innovations in this field, which may not be possible for everyone.
7. This method of teaching is costlier when compared to conventional teaching learning process.
8. Burden on teachers' is too much in this method as teacher should do systematic analysis of every content, standardize and present it to the students according to their ability and level of understanding.

Conclusion

Teacher is now called as a facilitator. The function of teacher is to extend facilities for children to learn and provide a suitable environment for it. The present day is very much relying on technology based education, that is presenting the knowledge to the students using computer/digital technology. It can be any electronic gadget that would make learning a bit different and interesting. It is to make the learning process a more of learner centered one. The task on part of teacher is very much, because teacher has to think different for every content and concept.

25

Utility and Challenges of Blended Learning

Introduction

Blended learning can be defined as the mixing of face-to-face teaching and online learning. Students have some choice over where they study (at school, at home or somewhere in between) and when they study (during school hours, in the evening or at weekends). But it is still the teacher who decides the extent of the choice, as well as which elements of the student's education are completed online and which elements are completed in the class.

Utilities of Blended learning

Under Utilities of blended learning, easier differentiation listed first order. With more time to work with individual students in class, teachers find they can better differentiate their teaching to suit individual needs, answering student questions and giving individual feedback. Many online resources also differentiate automatically: mathematics exercises can be set to get progressively harder the more answers a student gets right, for example. Blended models such as the flipped classroom use online videos and resources to prepare students before they come to class. This way, the students have already learnt the theory and can use the classroom time to put that theory into practice. In this model, the classroom teacher takes the role of guide and mentor and the results were more active students in that classroom.

There are thousands of online resources that enable students to create videos, animations, pod casts and new media. This gives our students new ways to engage with the work and express what they have learnt. Stronger students can also do extra work online to show their knowledge and understanding of a subject without taking up our valuable class time. Hence more creativity developed among the students.

Better prepared students

When the online work is done to prepare students in advance (in the flipped classroom model, for example), students arrive in class better prepared. This often means they are more engaged in the topic from the start.

Teaching 21st century skills

Today's students need to learn how to work study and collaborate online. They also need to develop the critical-thinking and creative skills demanded by modern employers. Blended learning helps us to teach these skills by encouraging our students to work share and collaborate online.

Less paperwork

Many teachers' desks and briefcases are full of student papers that need to be marked and returned. The grades and feedback also need to be logged in the students' grade book or report card. Online learning platforms digitize many assignments, so our marking can be done online (from school or at home).

All our teaching resources in one place

Online resources can be accessed from any internet-connected computer. This means we only have to upload a video, website link, newspaper article or other resource once. We and our students – as well as other teachers - will then be able to access it from their computers at home or internet-enabled computers in the PC lab.

Lower costs

Although setting up the IT required teaching blended learning may require some initial investment, many schools and colleges report reduced long-term costs due to reduced expenditure on textbooks, paper and photocopying.

Better informed parents

As most students do online work at home, this increases the opportunities for their parents to take part and help out. As a result, students get increased support from parents, and the parents feel a closer connection to their children's school work.

Getting discussions going in class

Every teacher would love their students to be enthusiastic about the topic they are about to teach before they enter the class. Online discussion forums are a simple way to get students thinking about a topic before a class. Anyone in the class can read and comment on contributions to the forum, and so start discussing the topic in advance. They are also useful as they give an opportunity for students who are not comfortable speaking in front of the class to take part in the discussion. Simply start by asking a question on the discussion forum, and then ask our students to contribute with their own thoughts, ideas, questions and online examples. As well as getting our students in the right frame of mind before the class, the comments on the forum will also give me a good idea of how many students know about a topic and what their opinions are (Nachimuthu, 2013).

Using Videos in Class and at Home

Many teachers would like to reduce the amount of talking they do in class to a minimum. This gives their students more opportunity to be active in class time, and gives the teacher more time to spend talking to and helping individual students. One answer is video. Often made by teachers, there are thousands of educational videos online, covering almost any subject from specific mathematics theories to ancient history? All we need to do is find the video, embed it (or just a link to it) into our learning platform, and ask our students to watch the video at home. They can watch the video to prepare before the class (watching it as many times as they need in order to understand it) and we can use our class time to discuss the video and complete exercises that practice the theory.

Social Media in a Safe Environment

Most students enjoy keeping in touch and sharing information using social media tools such as Face book, Twitter and You Tube. Learning platforms give us the chance to tap into this enthusiasm in a safe, school-controlled environment. One way to achieve this may be to create a shared resource page on our school's learning platform. Make the page not only accessible to all students but also editable by them, and they can then take ownership of the page by adding videos, comments, links and other materials themselves. In a geography class, for example, the resource page could cover a certain topic, such as glaciers (Vijayakumari, 2012). The students then gather as much information as they can about the topic and post it onto the resource page with a short explanation, and comment on the material posted by other students. If having one page for all student material seems disorganized, us can break the students into groups and ask each group to create a page.

Using Webcams for Revision

Letting students loose with webcams can aid the revision process – and take the weight off our shoulders. Blended learning gives us plenty of opportunities to encourage our students to get creative. Here's one way that we can engage their imaginations and simplify the revision process by using webcams. As we lead up to the end of term exam, divide our students into groups and ask each group to make a video that recaps a certain topic from the course. When all the videos have been completed, we can either show them in class or ask our students to watch them at home and give comments on a discussion forum. In this way, the videos become part of the shared resources of the class and everyone can watch them as they revise. Also, as the students know the videos will be reviewed by their classmates, they often work harder to make them right.

Research on students' learning in 'blended' environments has shown that they do some work online and some face-to-face. At best, students see a relation between these two, but they do not experience it as a seamless whole (e.g., Ellis, Goodyear, Calvo & Prosser, 2008). It would be risky to assume that teachers' experience 'blended' teaching as a unitary whole. (Akerlind, 2004).

Different Learning Methods

Different learning methods are engaged in the blended learning solutions. They are; self-paced e-learning; webinars (Broadcast style with large groups); virtual classrooms (with smaller groups); mobile learning; face-to-face training; one-to-one coaching (face-to-face); one-to-one coaching (telephone/web); access to learning resources; social learning (e.g. wikis, discussion forums); Action learning sets; project-based learning and assessment.

Conclusion

The myth about social media in the classroom is that if we use it, kids will be Tweeting, Face-booking and Snap-chatting while we're trying to teach. We still have to focus on the task at hand. We the teachers mistakenly thought that, *social media* for *socializing*. They're different; just as kids talking as they work in groups or talking while hanging out are different. Social media isn't exactly new, but its educational uses are still evolving. Many educators are able to use Twitter, Facebook, and blogs with their students, but other teachers find that their school districts block access to these and other social networking sites. Most would argue that social media, when used responsibly and appropriately by educators and students, has many uses in the classroom. Educators are using social media as a powerful tool for student learning, professional development, and to create and maintain personal learning networks.

The use of social media tools such as Facebook, Twitter, YouTube, Wikipedia, Edmodo, Ning, blogs, etc., provides students with a wider audience with whom they can share their ideas. At all times, students are expected to use the social media tools in a responsible manner and in support of the curriculum expectations being addressed. When students are able to safely share their ideas with an audience broader than just our classroom, they can often discover their voice and become even more motivated to learn, communicate, and share their ideas effectively with others. An additional outcome of our use of electronic communication and social media is to help students learn through experience, ways to safely use the Internet to share information and to collaborate.

For most teachers, blended learning does not save them time. But it does enable them to make better use of the limited time they have with their students. By moving some traditional classroom activities into the online world, we end up spending less time talking in front of the class and more time working with individual students.

References

1. Akerlind, G. S. (2004). A new dimension to understanding university teaching, Teaching in Higher Education, 9(3), 363-375.

2. Ashwin, P. (2006). Variation in academics' accounts of tutorials, Studies in Higher Education, 31(6), 651-665.

3. Carnell, E. (2007). Conceptions of effective teaching in higher education: extending the boundaries, Teaching in Higher Education, 12(1), 25-40.

4. Ellis,R.A.,Goodyear,P.,Calvo,R.A.,&Prosser,M.(2008).Engineering students' conceptions of and approaches to learning through discussions in face-to-face and online contexts. Learning and Instruction, 18(3), 267-282.

5. Nachimuthu, K .(2013). Attitude towards Multimedia Learning among Teacher Educators of Tamilnadu, Edu World, An International Journal of Education, APH pub, New Delhi,, Vol. 02., No.01., Jan-Dec.2013, pp.275-279.

6. Vijayakumari,G (2012). Perceptions on Multimedia technology by College of Education Teachers, EduLearn, Journal of Education and Learning, Vol.06., No.03., Aug-2012., Paper-V.

7. Trigwell,K., Prosser,M., Martin,E.,&Ramsden,P. (2005). University teachers' experiences of change in their understanding of the subject matter they have taught, Teaching in Higher Education, 10(2), 251-264.

26

Learning Environment of the Future Students

Introduction

In this condition, keeping the Learners with in a campus for long time will lead to a great loss of time and wealth. Hence, Open Learning concept has to be nurtured with enriched Quality. To, increase the quality of Learning in Open Learning; e- learning can be adopted. This article discusses about the blended platform- Open Leaning through e-learning. "An opportunity to design and build a Modern Learning Environment is an opportunity to create spaces fit for 21st century learners. As much as it's about buildings and furnishings, it's about creating spaces that promote learning that is personalised, student-centred, engaging and connected to real problems and the real world. Modern Learning Environments can help create the environment, mindsets and human capacity to help our young people make the most of their talents on the local and global stage. Students' learning needs have changed significantly.

New technologies and building materials allow for new, vibrant and well connected learning spaces. All students deserve to be taught in these new modern learning environments, and benefit from new teaching methods. For faster growth of the economy of a country human capital should be available along with physical capital. That is why, improving and expanding education are essential ingredients of any national development policy. However, developing countries fail to offer education to all sections of people in society through conventional on-campus system of education due to lack of infrastructural facilities and also some constraints embodied in it. Distance and open learning (ODL) system can play an important role to make-up this gap. In addition to allowing more students from different background, environments and geographical settings without requiring the uses of scarce on-site space, distance and open learning system also offers the educational institutions more revenue. That means, ODL system is a cost-effective way of mass education. On the other hand, especially in the developing countries, students who cannot go to school due to insolvent economic condition of the parents can have education by earning by themselves. So, ODL systems have proven themselves a way for people to gain education, which would otherwise not possible (Dekkers, 2000). However, when comparing with conventional forms o f education the provision of distance education requires considerably greater planning, larger upfront infrastructure costs and more complex student and administrative support systems (Lockwood, 1995; Rumble, 1986). Well-designed support systems facilitate the delivery of distance education courses of comparable quality and attrition rates to those for on-campus courses (NEA, 1999).

Open learning

Open learning is an innovative movement in education that emerged in the 1970s and evolved into fields of practice and study. The term refers generally to activities that either enhance learning opportunities within formal education systems or broaden learning opportunities beyond formal education systems. Open learning involves but is not limited to: classroom teaching methods, approaches to interactive learning, formats in work-related education and training, the cultures and ecologies of learning communities, and the development and use of open educational resources. While there is no agreed-upon, comprehensive definition of open learning, central focus is commonly placed on the "needs of the learner as perceived by the learner. " Case studies illustrate open learning as an innovation both within and across academic disciplines, professions, social sectors and national boundaries, and in business and industry, higher education institutions, collaborative initiatives between institutions, and schooling for young learners.

Open learning as a teaching method is founded on the work of Celestin Freinet in France and Maria Montessori in Italy, among others. Open learning is supposed to allow pupils self-determined, independent and interest-guided learning. A prominent example is the language experience approach to teaching initial literacy.

E-learning

E-learning (or eLearning) is the use of electronic media and information and communication technologies (ICT) in education. E-learning is broadly inclusive of all forms of educational technology in learning and teaching. E-learning is inclusive of, and is broadly synonymous with multimedia learning, technology-enhanced learning (TEL), computer-based instruction (CBI), computer managed instruction,[1] computer-based training (CBT), computer-assisted instruction or computer-aided instruction (CAI), internet-based training (IBT), web-based training (WBT), online education, virtual education, virtual learning environments (VLE) (which are also called learning platforms), m-learning, and digital educational collaboration. These alternative names emphasize a particular aspect, component or delivery method.

E-learning includes numerous types of media that deliver text, audio, images, animation, and streaming video, and includes technology applications and processes such as audio or video tape, satellite TV, CD-ROM, and computer-based learning, as well as local intranet/extranet and web-based learning. E-learning can occur in or out of the classroom. It can be self-paced, asynchronous learning or may be instructor-led, synchronous learning. E-learning is suited to distance learning and flexible learning, but it can also be used in conjunction with face-to-face teaching, in which case the term blended learning is commonly used.

Open Learning through e-Learning

The advantages of Open Learning and E-Learning can be combined to provide a Learner friendly plat form. There are several advantages and disadvantages with regards to motivation in Open Learning through e-learning. For many students, e-learning is the most convenient way to pursue a degree in higher education. A lot of these students are attracted to a flexible, self-paced method of education to attain their degree. It is important to note that many of these students could be working their way through college, supporting themselves or battling with serious illness. To these students, it would be extremely difficult to find time to fit college in their schedule. Thus, these students are more likely and more motivated to enroll in an e-learning class. Moreover, in asynchronous e-learning classes, students are free to log on and complete work any time they wish. They can work on and complete their assignments at the times when they think most cogently, whether it be early in the morning or late at night.

However, many teachers have a harder time keeping their students engaged in an e-learning class. A disengaged student is usually an unmotivated student, and an engaged student is a motivated student. One reason why students are more likely to be disengaged is that the lack of face-to-face contact makes it difficult for teachers to read their students' nonverbal cues, including confusion, boredom or frustration. These cues are helpful to a teacher in deciding whether to speed up, introduce new material, slow down or explain a concept in a different way. If a student is confused, bored or frustrated, he or she is unlikely to be motivated to succeed in that class.

Conclusion

To increase the quality of Learning in Open Learning; e-learning can be adopted. This article discusses about the blended platform-Open Leaning through e-learning. The existing Distance Education Institutions should adopt e-learning methodologies in imparting Learning to their students.

References

1. http://www.core-ed.org/professional-learning/modern-learning-resources
2. Koul, B.N., Singh, Baushise; Ansari, M. M. (ed) 1988. Studies in Distance education. New Delhi, AIU.
3. IGNOU (2008). Growth and Philosophis of D.E. New Delhi, Study material of PGDDE programme
4. Harichandan, D (1999). Open University System : A broad based attempt at Distance Education. University News, V0127 No. 36 pages 3-7, New Delhi, AIU.
5. http://en.wikipedia.org/wiki/E-learning#Pedagogical_approaches

27

Attitude of Blended Learning Among Student-Teachers

The ability of computers to present information visually is especially important for B.Ed. course. Well developed pictures, three dimensional s, animations and interactive environments allow easily understanding the learning objectives. The importance of using the computers is gradually increasing in terms of the course of B.Ed. In this information age, it is inevitable to witness technology use in educational settings. Teachers working in educational environments show great efforts to provide students with information by using effective technology - based methods. Parallel to these efforts, students become more qualified. In this way, students are supposed to be computer literate to obtain the information they need. In other words, with the use of educational technologies, learning becomes constant. Thus, most schools and Colleges in developed or developing countries try to adapt their education systems to communication technologies.

Research Studies

The investigators have reviewed few studies related to the topic under investigation. Fang, (2007) found this blended learning experience beneficial because they had the flexibility to learn at their own pace, reflect and recapitulate what was taught in class. They enjoyed this new learning experience and found it less stressful, as it allowed them to complete their work at any time. Condie & Livingston, (2007) suggested that students needed to be self-motivated and mature enough to learn in this mode. They also stated that teaching using a blended mode required new pedagogic skills. Boyle, (2005) findings suggested that participants still preferred the traditional teaching and learning approaches which is very different from the findings in much of the literature. Eugenia, (2010) the findings suggested that both groups of students had different preferences on blended learning approach and they preferred face-to-face meetings rather than online activities in general.

Need For the Study

This study could be beneficial for students as well as for institutions. The valuable Attitude towards Blended Learning s from 200 Student - Teachers should help to realize the benefit of this method in their education. Institutes can invest more learning facilities to enhance the performance of their students and produce better results. In this light, this research work has been determined to find out the level of Attitude towards Blended Learning. Hence the study is coined as ***"Attitude towards Blended Learning among Student - Teachers".***

Objectives of the Study

The major objective of the study is to find out the level of Attitude towards Blended Learning among Student – Teachers in Colleges of Education. The specific objective of the study is:

- o To find out the significant difference in the Mean scores on the level of Attitude towards Blended Learning among Student – Teachers with respect to the demographic variables such as Gender, Marital Status, Subject and Locality of the College.

Hypotheses of the Study

The hypotheses of the study arc

i.) The level of Attitude towards Blended Learning among Student – Teachers.

ii.) There is no significant difference in the Mean scores on the level of Attitude towards Blended Learning among Student – Teachers with respect to their demographic variables such as Gender, Marital Status, Subject and Locality of the College.

Methodology Of The Study

The present research study belongs to the Survey method, as the study aim only to measure the present level of the Attitude towards Blended Learning among Student - Teachers.

i) Selection and Size of the Sample

The investigator had selected 200 Student - Teachers as sample by Random Sampling Technique from Imayam College of Education, Jeevan College of Education and Kongunadu College of Education in Tiruchirappalli District.

ii) Tool Development

The investigator developed the tool for collecting data on the level of Attitude towards Blended Learning. It consists of 45 items with 4 point rating scale. They are Strongly Agree, Agree, Disagree and Strongly Disagree. The value of co-efficient of the reliability test is 0.83 found to be highly reliable. The tool was administered to the 200 Student - Teachers, after collecting the data the master table was prepared.

iii) Data Analysis

The investigator followed Mean, Standard deviation, 't' test and F test for the analysis of the data. The results were presented in the following tables.

Table – 1 : Mean and the Standard Deviation Scores on the Level of Attitude Towards Blended Learning Among Student-teachers in Total

S. No.	Variables		N	Mean	SD
1	Total		200	77.39	4.88
2	Gender	Male	103	75.81	4.45
		Female	97	79.07	4.78
3	Marital Status	Single	118	76.96	4.44
		Married	82	78.01	5.43
4	Subject	Arts	117	76.29	4.72
		Science	83	78.93	4.71
5	Locality of the College	Rural	119	66.22	5.14
		Urban	81	66.78	4.13

From the Table -1 it is that the obtained Maximum and Minimum Mean and SD values of the Attitude towards Blended Learning scores are 83.70 and 75.81; 5.43 and 2.72. It is also reveal that Mean and SD of the Attitude towards Blended Learning score of the total sample were 77.39 and 4.88. It shows that the level of Attitude towards Blended Learning among Student-Teachers is high.

Table – 2 : 't' Values in the Mean Scores on the Level of Attitude Towards Blended Learning Among Student-teachers With Respect to Their Gender

Gender	N	Mean	Std. Deviation	't' value
Male	103	75.81	4.45	4.98*
Female	97	79.07	4.78	

* - Significant at 0.05 level

From the above Table - 2 it is seen that the't' value, 4.98 is significant at 0.05 level. It is understood from the result that there is a significant difference in the level of Attitude towards Blended Learning with respect to their Gender. Female Student-Teachers are significantly having more level of Attitude towards Blended Learning than the Male Student-Teachers. Hence the framed null hypothesis is found to be rejected.

Table – 3 : 'T' Values in the Mean Scores on the Level of Attitude Towards Blended Learning Among Student-teachers With Respect to Their Subject

Gender	N	Mean	Std. Deviation	't' value
Arts	117	76.29	4.72	3.89*
Science	83	78.93	4.71	

* - Significant at 0.05 level

From the above Table - 3 it is seen that the't' value, 3.89 is significant at 0.05 level. It is understood from the result that there is a significant difference in the level of Attitude towards Blended Learning with respect to their Subject. Student-Teachers are studying in the Science subject are significantly having more level of Attitude towards Blended learning than the Student-Teachers are studying in the Arts subject. Hence the framed null hypothesis is found to be rejected.

Table – 4 : 'T' Values in the Mean Scores on the Level of Attitude Towards Blended Learning Among Student-teachers With Respect to Their Marital Status

Marital Status	N	Mean	Std. Deviation	't' value
Single	118	76.96	4.44	1.49**
Married	82	78.01	5.43	

** - Not Significant at 0.05 level

From the above Table - 4 it is seen that the't' value, 1.49 is not significant at 0.05 level. It is understood from the result that there is no significant difference in the level of Attitude towards Blended Learning with respect to their Marital Status. Single and Married Student-Teachers are having similar level towards Attitude towards Blended learning. Hence the framed null hypothesis is found to be accepted.

Table –5 : 'T' Values in the Mean Scores on the Level of Attitude Towards Blended Learning Among Student-teachers With Respect to Their Locality of the College

Locality of the College	N	Mean	Std. Deviation	't' value
Rural	119	66.22	5.14	0.85**
Urban	81	66.78	4.13	

** - Not Significant at 0.05 level

From the above Table - 5 it is seen that the't' value, 0.85 is not significant at 0.05 level. It is understood from the result that there is no significant difference in the level of Attitude towards Blended Learning with respect to their Locality of the College. Rural and Urban Colleges areas of Student-Teachers are having similar level towards Attitude towards Blended learning. Hence the framed null hypothesis is found to be accepted.

Findings of the Study

The findings of the present study are presented below. They are as followed

i. The level of Attitude towards Blended Learning among Student-Teachers is high.

ii. Female Student-Teachers are significantly having more level of Attitude towards Blended Learning than the Male Student-Teachers.

iii. Student-Teachers are studying in the Science subject are significantly having more level of Attitude towards Blended learning than the Student-Teachers are studying in the Arts subject.

iv. Single and Married Student-Teachers are having similar level towards Attitude towards Blended learning.

v. Rural and Urban Colleges areas of Student-Teachers are having similar level towards Attitude towards Blended learning.

Conclusion

From the research findings it is found that the Attitude towards Blended learning among the total Student – Teachers is high. It shows that the Student – Teachers are having more knowledge about Blended learning methods. The study also found that the Single and Married, Rural and Urban areas of Student – Teachers are having similar level towards Attitude towards Blended learning. Female Student-Teachers are significantly having more level of Attitude towards Blended Learning than the Male Student-Teachers. Student-Teachers are studying in the Science subject are significantly having more level of Attitude towards Blended learning than the Student-Teachers are studying in the Arts subject. These result shows that the Female Student-Teachers and Student-Teachers are studying in the Science subject Student - Teachers are having more collaborating methods to learning the subject matter. Hence it can be concluded that the Student - Teachers are having more level of Attitude towards Blended learning.

Reference

1. Boyle, T. (2005). A dynamic, systematic method for developing blended learning. Education, Communication and Information, Special Issue on Blended Learning, 5(3), 221-232.
2. Condie, R., & Livingston, K. (2007). Blending online learning with traditional approaches: Changing practices. British Journal of Educational Technology, 38(2), 337-348
3. Fang, L. (2007). Perceiving the useful, enjoyable and effective: A case study of the e-learning experience of tertiary students in Singapore. Educational Media International, 337-253(3), 237-253

28

Teaching Aptitude and Teaching Practice Among Teacher Educators

Introduction

This study aimed at the assessment of Blended Teaching Practice of Teacher Educators and its association with their Teaching Aptitude. The research article presented here is about Teacher Educators' experiences of teaching in blended learning environments. Blended learning environments are those where face-to-face, Self-Paced and online teaching-learning are combined which have become increasingly common in recent years. The survey method was used for the study. A Samples of 60 Teacher Educators from various colleges of Education from Madurai district were selected as the subjects for the study. Teaching Aptitude Test and Blended Teaching Practice inventory were constructed and used for data collection. The data was analyzed statistically. In this study it was found that there is negligible relationship between Teaching Aptitude and Blended Teaching Practice among the Teacher Educators.

Good planning of the teaching design and execution is vital for the success of any course. In today's current scenario of curriculum transaction there are many factors influencing the teaching learning process. Among those the two main factors i.e. the Teaching Aptitude and Method of teaching (Blended Teaching) is discussed in this article.

Aptitude

Individuals differ greatly in their gifts and capacities, such differences being both quantitative and qualitative. Aptitude refers to a natural or acquired capacity or ability especially a tendency, capacity or inclination to learn or understand (Webster's Medical Dictionary, 2002). It refers to part of a person's mental equipment which gives him a special fitness for any kind of endeavour. Such an aptitude may be the result of either an innate endowment or of special training or both. The mental and physical qualities giving rise to differences in aptitude are difficult to distinguish.

Teaching Aptitude

A variety of factors seems to go along with Teachers' Aptitude and is depended upon certain personal traits, intellectual and temperamental and these often will enable the teacher to get over even drastic constraints imposed on his performance. Teaching needs three qualities. Knowledge is the first, communication skill is the second, aptitude is the third (The Hindu, 2002, Sept. 3). Good teaching looks effortless because a teacher's knowledge and experience are invisible. Teaching is a tricky blend of action, a way of contextualising knowledge. Good teaching is, in fact, complex and challenging, and even the best teachers face difficulties translating formal knowledge into effective practice (Blase, 2006). A teacher with good teacher aptitude must be aware of the following essentials of teaching viz., plan a lesson, motivate students, curricular statements related, learning materials, teaching-learning strategies, essentials of the content, consolidation, elaborations, group activity, continuous and comprehensive evaluation, discipline, multi-level and multi grade activities, effective communication and interaction, etc. From the past to this technological era itself, a teacher has to enrich him/ her self in integrating technology to make the teaching blended.

Need for Blended Teaching

Blended Teaching is about effectively integrating ICTs into course design to enhance the teaching and learning experiences of students and teachers by enabling them to engage in ways that would not normally be available or effective in their usual environment, whether it is primarily face-to-face or distance mode. In many cases the act of "blending" achieves better student experiences and outcomes, and more efficient teaching and course management practices. It can involve a mix of delivery modes, teaching approaches and learning styles. Advances in technology provide new opportunities for teachers to design and deliver their courses in ways that support and enhance the teachers' role, the students' individual cognitive experiences, as well as the social environment; three key elements in successful learning and teaching. Blended learning technologies can:

1. Broaden the spaces and opportunities available for learning;
2. Support course management activities (e.g., communication, assessment submission, marking and feedback);
3. Support the provision of information and resources to students;
4. Engage and motivate students through interactivity and collaboration.

So it is not just about using technology because it is available; blended learning is about finding better ways of supporting students in achieving the learning objectives and providing them with the best possible learning and teaching experiences, as well as supporting teachers in their role (including the management and administration of courses). Of course, the integration of blended learning in courses will naturally vary according to such factors as: discipline, year level, student characteristics and needs, course or program learning objectives, as well as the academic's approach to teaching, and confidence and experience in using technology.

Blended Teaching Modes

Blended teaching spans a continuum that covers a wide range of activities between conventional face-to-face interactions and those that are fully online. Griffith's Blended Teaching Strategy identifies three modes of operation to indicate the level of use of technology in learning and teaching.

Mode 1: Technology is used to facilitate course management and resources for learner support. For example, to provide information and resources to students (e.g., lecture notes or recordings, assessment guidelines), and to perform basic administrative functions (e.g., announcements or course emails).

Mode 2. Technology is used to enrich the quality of the student learning experience through interactive learning activities beyond those attainable through face-to-face classroom interactions. For example, utilizing technology wherever necessary to support communication and collaboration, assessment and the management of the course along with regular lectures.

Mode 3: Technology is used to support learning that is largely self-directed but also involves the use of interactive and collaborative learning activities. In this mode courses are delivered fully online. The present study is an attempt to estimate the extent of relationship of Teaching Aptitude with Blended Teaching

Practice among the Teacher Educators in the field of teacher education.

Objectives

1. To measure the level of Teaching Aptitude and Blended Teaching Practice among the Teacher Educators in Madurai district.
2. To find out the significant difference in the Teaching Aptitude among the Teacher Educators in terms of the attributive variables viz. Gender, Age, Educational Qualification, Nature of the Institution, Marital Status, Internet Usage and Area of the residence.
3. To find out the significant difference in the Blended Teaching Practice among the Teacher Educators in terms of the attributive variables viz. Gender, Age, Educational Qualification, Nature of the Institution, Marital Status, Internet Usage and Area of the residence.
4. To find out the relationship between Teaching Aptitude and Blended Teaching Practice among the Teacher Educators in Madurai district.

Hypothesis

1. The level of Teaching Aptitude and Blended Teaching Practice among the Teacher Educators in Madurai district is not satisfactory.
2. There is no significant difference in the Teaching Aptitude among the Teacher Educators in terms of the attributive variables viz. Gender, Age, Educational Qualification, Nature of the Institution, Marital Status, Internet Usage and Area of the residence.
3. There is no significant difference in the Blended Teaching Practice among the Teacher Educators in terms of the

attributive variables viz. Gender, Age, Educational Qualification, Nature of the Institution, Marital Status, Internet Usage and Area of the residence.

4. There is no relationship between Teaching Aptitude and Blended Teaching Practice among the Teacher Educators in Madurai district.

Sample

For this study 60 Teacher Educators from Eight Colleges of Education in Madurai district affiliated to Tamil Nadu Teachers' Education University, Chennai were selected randomly as sample.

Tools used for the study

There are two tools used in the study which are constructed by the researcher. They are 1. Teaching Aptitude Test which consists of 30 statements and 2.Blended Teaching Practice Inventory comprising of 30 items including 19 positive statements and 11 negative statements. They have 'Yes' and 'No' as options where Yes carries one mark and No carries Zero mark for positive items and the reverse for negative items.

Table 1: Teaching Aptitude and Blended Teaching Practice level of Teacher Educators

Variable	Sample samples	Number of mean	Theoretical mean	Obtained
Teaching Aptitude	Teacher Educators	60	15	26.42
Blended Teaching Practice	Teacher Educators	60	15	13.96

From the above table No.1 it is quite evident that the obtained mean for Teaching Aptitude is 26.42 which are greater than the theoretical mean 15 and the obtained mean for Blended Teaching Practice is 13.96 which are lesser than the theoretical mean. Hence the framed null hypothesis is partially accepted.

Table 2 : Difference in Teaching Aptitude and Blended Teaching Practice

				Teaching Aptitude		Blended Teaching Practice	
S.No	**Variables**	**Category**	**N**	**'t' value**	**Level of Significance**	**'t' value**	**Level of Significance**
1.	Gender	Male	19	0.45	**N.S**	0.93	**N.S**
		Female	41				
2.	Age	Below 30	11	0.76	**N.S**	0.49	**N.S**
		Above 30	49				
3.	Educational Qualification	M.Phil	40	0.34	**N.S**	0.21	**N.S**
		NET/Ph.D	20				
4.	Nature of Institution	Govt.Aided	23	1.21	**N.S**	1.24	**N.S**
		Self Finance	37				
5.	Marital Status	Married	45	0.15	**N.S**	0.07	**N.S**
		Unmarried	15				
6.	Internet Usage	Daily	29	0.12	**N.S**	2.18	**S**
		Rarely	31				
7.	Area of Residence	Urban	42	0.25	**N.S**	2.12	**S**
		Rural	18				

*S – Significant *NS – Not Significant *Table 't' value = 1.96 at 0.05 level of significance

The table No.2 indicates that there is no significant difference in the Teaching Aptitude among the Teacher Educators in terms of the attributive variables viz. Gender, Age, Educational Qualification, Nature of the Institution, Marital Status, Internet Usage and Area of the residence. This shows that the teaching Aptitude is high for the sample. Hence the framed Null hypothesis is fully accepted. Hence the framed null hypothesis is fully accepted.

For the variable Blended Teaching Practice there is no significant difference among the Teacher Educators in terms of the attributive variables viz. Gender, Age, Educational Qualification, Nature of the Institution and Marital Status, Significant difference is seen for the variables Internet Usage and Area of the residence. This shows that the Blended Teaching Practice is low among the Teacher Educators in general and seems to be high for those who use internet regularly and for the sample residing in urban area. Hence the framed null hypothesis is partially accepted.

Table 3 : Relationship between Teaching Aptitude and Blended Teaching Practice among Teacher Educators.

S. No.	**Variables**		**N**	**Calculated 'r' Value**	Correlation
1.	Teaching Aptitude	Blended Teaching Practice	60	0.018	Slightly, almost negligible relationship

From the above table No.3 it is inferred that the level of Teaching Aptitude has slightly, almost negligible relationship with Blended Teaching Practice among teacher educators because this may be due to the reason that the blending of various methods of teaching is inevitable but there are lot of problems in practical implementation even though the teacher educators have high level of Teaching Aptitude.

Blended Teaching Possibilities

The term 'Blended Teaching' nowadays primarily means integrating the use of technology in course design and delivery.

Taking a blended learning approach to our course can be used to support face-to-face teaching, large group and small group learning, self-directed learning, communication between the teacher and individual students or groups of students, as well as between students themselves. We can "blend" ***time*** (e.g., face-to-face vs. recorded lectures), ***place*** (small group tutorial on-campus vs. online discussion forum; traditional field trip vs. 'virtual' field trip using web sites and online chat with industry personnel), ***people*** (podcast of guest lecturers, or virtual classroom to include both on-campus and off-campus students), ***resources*** and ***activities*** (textbook vs. online readings; in-class vs. online quiz).

Implementation

Good practice in blended teaching doesn't necessarily mean adopting a wide range of technologies for a particular course. It can mean simply using a few tools, but in effective ways in order to achieve quality in teaching, learning and/or course management. For example, a teacher may upload lecture notes (and perhaps lecture recordings) on their course site, regularly use the announcement and email functions, and include other information and resources on their course site, online submission of Assignments, etc. However, the teacher may also integrate the use of a discussion board in their course design, including a number of different forums such as a Question and Answer forum between teacher and students, an informal 'students only' forum, as well as a number of topic forums relating to different components of the course where students are required to post comments that form part of the assessment task/s.

Designing for blended teaching requires a systematic approach, starting with:

1. **Planning** for integrating blended teaching into the course, followed by;
2. **Designing** and **developing** the blended learning elements;

3. **Implementing** the blended learning design to the students;
4. **Reviewing** (evaluating) the effectiveness of blended teaching design, and finally;
5. Planning for the next delivery of the course then involves **improving** the blended teaching - learning experience for both staff and students.

Suggestions

As per the results obtained in this study the Teacher Educators possess high level of teaching aptitude but low level of Blended Teaching practice, which may be due to so many reasons as per the individual's interest, ability, environment, etc. The researcher is giving few suggestions to come out with effective blended teaching practices as part and parcel of our Teacher Education system. They are

1. NCTE has instructed to establish an Educational Technology Lab in all Colleges of Education and most of the labs are not fully furnished with the facilities such as Internet connection, Ear phone, Web camera, Smart board, etc.
2. The curriculum should be designed in order to enhance blended teaching - learning environment by making it compulsory to handle (content, resources, activities, assessment) at least few units in each paper through Blended teaching.
3. University can conduct Orientation programmes (can be in 5 main centers) for teacher educators (working under both Government aided and Self-financing stream) to enrich their practical knowledge for the usage and integration of technology in their day-to-day teaching. Also this will help them to come out of Technophobia where many suffer from.

4. The management should motivate the teacher educators to teach in a blended way and also should grant provision and accessibility for the needed facilities for staff and students.

5. Awareness programmes could be conducted to the student teachers to learn through Online schedules, Technology Literacy, Handling the Technological problems, etc.

6. Guidance should be given to student teachers to use the technology resources in the Right place, for the Right purpose, at the Right time, through the Right way without wasting their Time, Money and Energy and only for the expansion of their knowledge and not for mere entertainment.

7. Teacher Educators should develop a positive mentality to accept the student teachers' feedbacks about the blended way of teaching. This will help the teacher educators to plan and frame an updated and effective blended teaching modes for the next set of students.

8. Teacher educators can create their own blog, discussion forum, webcast, polling, pod cast, online quizzes, social book marking, etc.

Conclusion

Teacher educators should develop their Aptitude to update themselves along with the upcoming technologies teaching methods. The process of blended teaching- learning should also be observed so that teacher educators can make necessary adjustments and suggestions, thus enabling students to utilize their own skills and achieve their common learning goals. Therefore, good preparation and decision-making is essential not only for efficient use of time in the construction and maintenance of their resources, but also for the creation of quality learning experiences for their students.

References

1. John w best and James V. khan (1992), "Research in Education", Prentice Hall of India pvt. Ltd. New Delhi.
2. Kothari C. R (1995), "Research Methodology Methods and Techniques", Wiley eastern Limited, New Delhi.
3. http://www.griffith.edu.au/__data/assets/pdf_file/0007/197143/BlendedLearningStrategy.pdf
4. https://intranet.secure.griffith.edu.au/computing/blended-learning-support
5. http://www.griffith.edu.au/__data/assets/pdf_file/0006/180879/Blended-Learning-Imp-Plan-FINAL_May09.pdf

29

Awareness Towards Utilizing Cell Phones For Students

Introduction

The invention of the fixed telephone in the late 19th century in the United States changed the way that people interacted and communicated. This has been paralleled in the early 21st century by the advent of the mobile phone. The mobile phone was originally created for business use. In the last few years extraordinary growth has taken place worldwide Information and Communication Technologies (ICT) and especially in the ICT sector tied to mobile communications, as evidenced by the more than two billion mobile phones handsets sold around the world in 2013. Mobile and light weight devices that are sometimes small enough to fit in a pocket or in the palm of one's hand are part of everyday life.

Mobile Learning

Nine in ten people (more than 5 billion individuals) around the world are carrying a powerful computing device in their pockets and purses. They don't realize it, but today's mobile phones have the computing power of a personal computer from the mid-nineties, while consuming a fraction of the energy and are made at significantly lower cost. In India, the mobile phone has revolutionized communication and India is now one of the faster growing markets for mobile phone service, with growing usage and increasing penetration. According to TRAI, there are 286 million wireless subscribers in India, June 2008, of which 76 million were capable of accessing data service. The increasing ubiquity of the mobile phone begs for it to be used as a learning tool.

Mobile Internet Browsers

Internet browsers are now built into an increasing number of phones, especially those that take advantage of 3G or enhanced data networks such as GPRS. Having a browser on the phone opens up all the learning resources available on the web, including Google, LMS applications, typical e-learning courseware and other tools/applications.

M-learning in India

The Biju Patnaik University of Technology started a service in collaboration with SMS Gup Shup called the BPUTALERT, which distributes information, academic notice and calendars through SMS to students. Voice tap is another service using which people can send their queries through SMS, and the company messages back names of experts on the subject, and then users can connect to the right expert. The field mobile learning is in its infancy, and developers are still fumbling with products.

Mobile Communication Between Parents, Teachers and Students

The new mobile technologies can be used in mediate the relationships between schools and parents. The discourses of the participants for what regards the new mobile technologies have been analyzed in order to mediate the relationships between the school and the parents, leaving the possibility of discussing more general topic to the parent school relationship.

Scope of the Study

1. To Study the attitude of teenagers towards cellular phones.
2. Enumerate the usage patterns and arrive at peculiarities.
3. Examine the way young people relate to the functionality of mobile phones as well as asses observable phenomena.

In this context the investigator attempts to study the influence and awareness towards utilizing cell phones among the higher secondary school students.

Need of the Study

Most of the people are using mobile phones in their daily life. Mobile phones are using to send the message and communicate the information's easily. Also college students are using the mobile for clearing the doubts on their subjects from teachers and pears. Hence this study is most important to identify the awareness of the mobile phones among the higher secondary school students.

Review of Literature

According to Guerra (2007), although most of the people are frequent textures, not all of them apply shorthand texting when writing. She said that students say it does affect their writing proficiency, and it has no impact at all. Nevertheless, texting is still a problem to most people. Edwards (2009) said that texting contributes to people's indolence when it comes to writing. In his own experience, he himself developed changes on his writing abilities ever since he engaged in text messaging. According to him, it helps in speeding up communication. And because of frequent usage of shortened messages in texting, it becomes a "habit". He sometimes caught himself using the shorthand method of writing even in doing his projects in school, which goes to show that text messaging has really affected his writing ability. When he researched in the internet, he discovered that many people also believed that texting affects the writing skills of students. Edwards always feel that using the "original way" of writing when doing his school project is more difficult than using the "text messaging language". Because of this, he became lazier. He also said that most people are hooked up to texting that they send text messages even when they're doing several activities like driving, when in a funeral, or in a graduation ceremony.

Myhra (2010) concluded that frequent sending of text messages could affect the student's way of writing. Students have developed the habit of writing in shorthand form, which caused them to write informally. Texting has affected the students writing and grammar proficiency negatively.

Objectives of the Study

1. To find out the level of significant difference between Boys and Girls higher secondary school students among the awareness towards utilizing Cell phones.
2. To find out the level of significant difference between Rural and Urban higher secondary school students among the awareness towards utilizing Cell phones.
3. To find out the level of significant difference between Government, Government Aided and Private higher secondary school students among the awareness towards utilizing Cell phones.

Hypothesis of the Study

The null hypotheses were made with above objectives of the study.

Methodology

Normative survey method was used for the present study.

Samples For the Study

The investigator used random sampling technique for the selection of sample. 160 students were selected as sample of the present study. Out of these 160 students 75 of them are boys and 85 of them are girls.

Tool Used For the Study

To assess the awareness of utilizing cell phones among the students the tool ATUCP (Awareness towards Utilizing Cell Phones) was consists of 50 statements with four point rating scale was used. This was developed and standardized by the investigator.

Scoring Procedure

The students were asked to show their responses by placing (✓) tick marks. The tool consists of 28 positive statements and 22 negative statements. The negative statements were scored as 1/2/3/4 and positive statements were scored as 4/3/2/1 they are Strongly Agree, Agree, Disagree and Strongly Disagree.

Statistical techniques used

For the analysis of data following statistical techniques were adopted. They were,

i) Arithmetic Mean
ii) Standard Deviation and
iii) 't'-test

Analysis of the Data

The result of the Analyzed Data is presented below.

Table–1 : Significant difference between Boys and Girls higher secondary school students' on the Awareness towards utilizing cell phones

Gender	N	Mean	S.D	't' Value	Significance at 0.05 Level
Boys	75	77.85	7.07	1.56	1.97**
Girls	85	79.70	7.84		

**No Significant

The above table-1 shows that the calculated't' value is less than the tabulated't' value at 0.05 level of significance. Hence the null hypothesis is accepted, so there is no significant difference between Boys and Girls higher secondary school students' on the awareness towards utilizing cell phones.

Table–2 : Significant difference between Rural and Urban higher secondary school students on the Awareness towards utilizing cell phones.

Locality	N	Mean	S.D	't' Value	Significance at 0.05 Level
Rural	90	77.72	8.35	2.09	1.97*
Urban	70	80.07	6.12		

* Significant

The above table-2 shows that the calculated 't' value is more than the tabulated 't' value at 0.05 level of significance. Hence the null hypothesis is not accepted. So there is significant difference between Rural and Urban higher secondary school students on the awareness towards utilizing cell phones.

Table–3 : Significant difference between Government and Private higher secondary school students on the Awareness towards utilizing cell phones

Types of School	N	Mean	S.D	't' Value	Significance at 0.05 Level
Government	50	75.70	9.05	3.77	1.98*
Aided	50	81.50	6.02		
Aided	50	81.50	6.02	1.82	1.98**
Private	60	79.35	6.32		
Private	60	79.35	6.32	2.41	1.98*
Government	50	75.70	9.05		

* Significant ** No Significant

The above table-3 shows that the Government and Aided schools students and Government and Private schools students are differed on the awareness towards utilizing cell phones. But Aided and Private schools students 't' value is less than the table value. So there is no significant difference between Aided and Private Students.

Major Findings of the Study

1. There is no significant difference between Boys and Girls and Aided and Private Higher Secondary School Students on the awareness towards utilizing Cell phones.

2. There is significant difference between Rural and Urban, Government and Aided and Private and Government Higher Secondary School Students on the awareness towards utilizing Cell phones.

Discussion

1. Awareness towards Utilizing Cell phones are more by the Girls than the Boy Students. Because, the Girls are more enthusiastic to work and use of cell phones.
2. Awareness towards Utilizing Cell phones are more by the Urban students than the Rural students. Because, the Urban students are having more opportunities to use the Cell phones. But, the Rural students are having less opportunities to use the Cell phones.
3. Awareness towards Utilizing Cell phones are more among Aided and Private School students. Because most of the Aided and Private Schools are mostly connected with the Parents on the progress, fees, results, attendance and relevant information's. So they have more awareness than the Government School students.
4. Regarding the review of literature past research's are in using the cell phones. But this research is known about awareness on the utilizing cell phones. So it is different from the review and the results are also new one.

Educational Implication of the Study

1. More measures are to be taken at Rural and Government School Students to create awareness of utilizing cell phones.
2. More programmes are to be conducted to create awareness of using cell phones for the benefit of higher secondary school students, parents and teachers.
3. The Teachers may be trained to teach their lessons by using the cell phones.
4. Government should introduce the curriculum about awareness of utilizing cell phones.

Conclusion

In the past three years, we have gone from a smattering of mobile to an abundance of useful information. But there's still a long way to go, there are still huge gaps in our knowledge to utilize the cell phones. It has been predicted that by the end of 2014 the number of mobile phone users in India will reach 1 billion. In the world every 100 citizens 97 are have mobiles. In India 90.47 have mobiles. In future M - teaching and learning is a new creative approach and technique to apply in Education for futuristic developments and requirements of the society.

References

1. Cruse, Alan D. (2000). Meaning in Language: An Introduction to Sematics and Pragmantics. United States: Oxford University Press Inc.
2. Quattrini,J.A.(1985).Brushing Up Your Writing Skills. 215 Park Avenue South, New York, N.Y.10003: Arco Publishing, Inc.
3. Montiel, C.J. and Estuar, M.R.(2006), Revolutionary Text: Social Psychology of Cell phone Texting during People Power II. Ateneo de Manila University.
4. Shidle, N.(1965).The Art of Successful Communication, USA: McGraw-Hill, Inc.
5. Edwards, Corban. (2009).Text Messaging Effects on Writing. Retrieved December 31, 2010 from htt://personal.georgiasouthern.edu/~ce00988/.
6. Guerra, Nicole.(2007) Texting Affects Student Writing: R U Concerned?. Rettrieved January 6, 2011 from http://gnovisjournal.org/blog/text-based-short-hand-affecting-teens-writing-r-u-concerned.

7. Myhra, John.(2010).Negative Effects of Texting in the Classroom. Retrieved January 21, 2011 from http://www.56wrtg1150.wikidot.com/ negative-effects-of-texting-in-the-classroom.

8. http://www.newsflash.org/2002/06/si/si001247.hum

9. https://bora.uib.no/bitstream/1956/3320/1/56404526.pdf

10.http://www.csudh.edu/psych/lrosen.htm.

11.http://www.etec.hawaii.edu/proceedings/2009/Tomita.pdf.

30

Cloud Computing

Introduction

Computers are scientific device that can help us in solving human problems. Human problems are increasing day by day as scientific inventions are increased. Computers are machines. They are created and managed by men. Computers have no brain of their own. But it is invented by human brain. Anything they do is the result of human instructions. They carry out instructions whether it is wrong or right. However modern computers are generating tremendous work beyond human comprehension. We have systems on our studying table. We operate and we are able to get needed information from a centre as Earth gets water from the cloud. So, we consider clouds as the mother of earth. Such as cloud computer centre is being considered a store house of knowledge and information. Here we are going to analyze the merits and demerits of using 'cloud in the field of Education.

Stone age to digital age

During the age of starting human race, man used only rough stones for their all purposes. Even they used small stones for calculations. Mathematics plays a vital role in all walks of human life. Cooking to coding, plants to planets, eating to evaluation, we need calculations and they are based on calculations only that too calculate very quickly, quick decision and quick solution are urgently needed in this scientific world. Population is increased and so needs are also increased. To meet the needs of mankind every steps are to be calculated in agriculture, industrial, and judicial, educational etc., our age is scientific world. Science turned the world top to bottom. Even we can call our age computer age. The wide world has shrinked to a global village or even global family. We can get any news or any incidents taken place in a corner of the world is known within a fraction of the seconds by everybody. It is possible by utilizing internet and computers. Webs or nets are numerous. Amazon cloud computing is one among them.

Types of cloud computing

A cloud is a collection of water drops and particles. So cloud computing also a place or a centre where a lot of sources and data and all sorts of information's are all can be stored for to get by the needier. It acts as a library or a departmental store where we can get or purchase as per our need. This AMAZON is one of best centers among a lot. It has four divisions or four sections. They are:

1. Infrastructure- IAAS- Infrastructure As A Service
2. Plat form- PAAS-Plat Form As Service
3. Software – SAAS-Software As A Service
4. Storage- SAAS-Storage As A Service

The type or the title itself denotes the services of the cloud. We have one system. But, we need a infrastructure for a college construction which we do not know. At this time, to save money and time we can get all the information's from the cloud computing. So as we can collect all needs from it with the permission of the higher authority of 'AMAZON' centre. We may consider it as a big library also.

How to operate?

In formations and inventions which are stored in this centre should not be misused. It is a transaction between the user and the server. They cannot be fooled or the information are theft or Now the working speed has been increased i.e. 8GB to 500 MB. That speed should not be interrupted by any of the distraction. Short routers and cheating minds should not be allowed. So, there are a lot of merits in it as well as demerits. Computers students may try to resolve this problem in making log in system with secret passwords. That day will soon come. Let us hope positively.

Cloud computing in education world/Field

1. Education is the manifestation of perfection already in man.
2. Knowledge is power
3. Education is eye of human being
4. All lands and places belong to learned persons
5. The learning acquired in one birth helps a man in seven rebirths.
6. The wealth which have declines is education

Considering the above statements, we come to know the importance of education So education is a must to all human beings.

The Question is how to get and acquire the knowledge and perishes education. It has three phases.

1. Teachers
2. Students
3. Teachings.

Education is endless process. Teachers are learned persons. They should learn and going on learn. He should be a master of his subject and know something about all subjects. He has to teach any subjects in an innovative way using some techniques, with some tools and aids. Now a days computer takes that part and it plays a big part. Teacher has to program a unit and display in screen or by a way of power point presentation. When the teacher is not in a position to explain all the facts of a unit, he has to borrow from so body else. Hence he goes to clouds and gets the in formations. So, storage e, network, localization are neither related nor easy to approach and get very fast them to feed the students. It is more effective and attractive way of teaching. The next place occupies by students or learners. They see, follow and learn things. Whenever doublets arise they clarify, discuss with the teachers. In this mechanical world, everything is solved by machine and hardware. Students Co-operation interest and involvement are needed. Teacher is hardly a mediator or agent only. Third place goes to teaching.

Teaching is what to teach, when to teach and how to teach and whom to teach are to be planed and prepared. The new kind of teaching demands teachers to the digital content or E-content materials. Hence the teacher educations are to learn this E-content, innovate ideas to develop the students for employability.

We have 32 teaching techniques in our Tamil classical grammar books. We wonder when we read those techniques. Those techniques may be applied in our teaching process through computer in this digital age. The time is now to think behind digital age. Tremendous charges are taken place in our day to-day life. Lifestyle is mostly changed. Our dress, food habit, transports and what else, everything is changed we have to go with the speed change of the world even in teaching process also. Our objective is,

1. To promote our generation to a creative society.
2. To generate employment for younger generation.
3. To create new techniques in teaching for the better teaching.
4. To fulfill the necessary requirements of the society.
5. To develop the nation in promoting all fields of overall developments.
6. To eradicate poverty, ignorant and disparity.
7. To generate unity, equality and generosity.

Conclusion

Dear friends, we have assembled here to discuss and create a new concept based on clouds computing in teaching, learning processor fitting to the Digital Age. Our scholars prepare curriculum and syllabus to applicable to age group of students. Government allots a lump of money for education we, the teachers are the agents between the students and the government. We are well paid. It is our duty to fulfill the aspiration of the students and aim of the government. We should take a pledge that we will do our best service with involvement and dedication in our noble profession. Let us look for war, join lands and lead the society to the digital age- even beyond, this by utilizing 'clouds'. In this process our youth may find some novel way how to correct errors, avoid misuses end and ensure our best services for the better world. Thanks for the very good opportunities given to me by the 'TNTE' University.

References

1. www.ibm.com/developerworks/websphere/zones/hipods/library.html\
2. http://communication.howstuffworks.com/cloud-computing2.html
3. www.thbs.com
4. http://www.wikipedia.org/

31

Effectiveness of E-content in Teaching

Introduction

The development of Science and Technology, especially the application of information and communication technology (ICT) in the new era has greatly influenced teaching and learning in education. The issue of information and communication technology (ICT) in teaching apparently facilitates both the effort of the teacher as well as the learner. In the present era of knowledge explosion, adopting modern tools for teaching is one of the predominant needs of the hour. Knowledge packaging in electronic form or e-content is a powerful technique for teaching all subjects. ICT have become handy in class room teaching which has the potential to engage the students throughout the period and make learning easy and effective through, visual aids, animations and simulations. They will be able to see the different stages and functions of the learning object which they cannot normally see through naked eyes the repeatability or reusability of technology based learning system meets the needs of all the differently capable students to understand better. Therefore the technology based teaching and learning has become essential. The term 'e-content' refers to that form of knowledge or content which is packed in an electronic form. It includes text, audio, video, animations, images etc. The major findings of the present study are: An Achievement test was conducted for validating the developed e-content to access the effectiveness of the e-content. While analyzing the result, i.e., the performance of the student teachers in the achievement test is better and it became clear that the e-content is effective. While administering the e-content to the student teachers, which is a self-instructional learning strategy it is found that e-content promotes active participation and encourages vigilance. It was found that learning through e-content and learning through traditional lecture method are not similar and they differ significantly.

The development of Science and Technology, especially the application of information and communication technology (ICT) in the new era has greatly influenced teaching and learning in education. In the present era of knowledge explosion, adopting modern tools for teaching is one of the predominant needs of the hour. Instructional technology in the third world is changing rapidly. Knowledge packaging in electronic form or e-content is a powerful technique for teaching all subjects. ICT have become handy in class room teaching which has the potential to engage the students throughout the period and make learning easy and effective through, visual aids, animations and simulations.

Need For the Study

New innovations are coming to the fields of education in terms of technology which promises to change the process of teaching and learning. Training of competent teachers is very important because they directly or indirectly influence the quality and the quantity of educational services. Without adequately trained teacher cadre the institution cannot aim to expand the educational facilities.

E-content

The term 'e-content' refers to that form of knowledge or content which is packed in an electronic form. It includes text, audio, video, animations, images etc. An innovative application of computer in the teaching and learning process is e-content. E-content is the advancement of technology to design, deliver, select, administer and extend learning.

Objectives of the Study

1. To prepare e-content for particular topic in Teaching of Biological Science Education at B.Ed., level.
2. To find out whether there is any significant difference in achievement means score between control group and experimental group in learning Teaching of Biological Science Education by the B.Ed., student teachers.

Methodology

The investigator followed the experimental method for the present study. The data thus collected were put into appropriate statistical analysis: Mean, t-test, standard deviation.

Sampling Procedure

The present study is concerned only with B.Ed student teachers in J.J. College of Education and Oxford College of Education, Trichy. Hence the college selected could be considered as a representative college. Eighteen students have been selected for experimental group and another eighteen students for control group by using purposive sampling method.

Hypotheses of the Study

The following hypotheses were formulated based on the objectives of the study:

1. There is no significant difference in the Posttest achievement mean scores between control group and experimental group.
2. There is significant difference in the achievement mean scores between the Pre and Post test of experimental groups who learnt through e-content.

Table – 1 : The table shows the comparison of Post-test achievement mean scores of Experimental group and control group.

Locality	N	Mean	S.D	't' Value	df	Level of Significance
Control Group	18	8.72	1.127	9.22	34	
Experimental Group	18	13.33	1.910			Significant

The calculated t-value 9.22 is greater than the critical value 2.704 corresponding to the 0.01 level of significance. This implies that the control group and experimental group differ significantly in their achievement in the post-test. Hence the null hypothesis is not accepted.

Table – 2 : The table shows the difference between the Pre-test and Post-test achievement mean scores due to treatment for the experimental group.

Experimental Group	No of student	Mean	S.D	't' Value	df	Level of Significance
Pre – test	18	10.72	1.364	8.040	34	Significant
Post - test	18	13.33	1.910			

The calculated t-value 8.040 is greater than the critical value 2.704 corresponding to the 0.01 level of significance. This shows that experimental group is highly significant in their achievement in post-test. Hence the null hypothesis is accepted.

Major Findings of the Study

The major findings which have emerged from the study are as follows:

1. An Achievement test was conducted to access the effectiveness of the e-content. While analyzing the result, i.e., the performance of the students in the achievement test is better and it became clear that the e-content is effective.

2. The student teachers of experimental group who were taught through e-content achieved more in subject units than the control group student teachers.

3. It was found .that learning through e-content and learning through traditional lecture method are not similar and they differ significantly.

Educational Implications of the Study

1. New instructional techniques of assisting student through computer are to be explored by the teachers and researchers continuously.

2. Teachers of higher secondary schools can be given orientation as how to develop e-content.

3. The use of e-content is found to be valid in enhancing the achievement; it will diminish wastage and stagnation in school.

Conclusion

Based on the proceeding findings of the study, the following conclusions are arrived. The levels of performance of teacher trainees who learnt through e-content were greater the other part and hence it was evident that e-content is also an effective approach to teach Biological Science Education. The rise of e-learning and an electronic content (e-content) is a new paradigm for education and training in the knowledge society, empowered by technological advancements which give the modern instructional technology. The development of educational content in time with the changing times has become a major responsibility of the modern teacher who has to face a new learner in a new environment.

References

1. Amutha. S. & Ramganesh. E e-content- An Inevitable Supplement for a Teacher Educator. Paper presented at the *International conference on Quality Enhancement in Distance Education for Lifelong Learning* 26-27 March 2011, Edited by Dr.K.Anandhan, Bharathidasan University.
2. Jeya Shanmuga Raja. J, E-Content Development on Teaching method of Zoology at B.Ed Level., Paper presented at the *International conference on Quality Enhancement in Distance Education for Lifelong Learning* 26-27 March 2011, Edited by Dr.K.Anandhan, Bharathidasan University.
3. Suma.S.(2007). Development and Validation of e-content on the uses of the simple present tense in English at higher secondary level. M.Phil Thesis submitted to Bharathidasan University.

32

Blended Learning in Teacher Education

Introduction

The rapid and sustainable progress in the field of science and technology has radically changed our Educational scenario. . If learning is to have the level of quality that we dream for it, we as educators need to proactively be a part of the Blended Learning that is inevitably coming our way. Teachers must be an active part of designing online learning's rigor and quality or they will be left in the dust. Lifco dictionary states blend means, mix together different kinds of substances. We live in a world in which technological innovation is occurring at break-neck speed and digital technologies are increasingly becoming an integral part of our day-to-day lives. Therefore, it is essential to blend our learning through various pathways. The role of teachers in Blended Learning is very prominent in improving the reasoning and creativity skill of the students.

The rapid and sustainable progress in the field of science and technology has radically changed our Educational scenario.

Teacher education institutions now encounter Generation Y learners at present and it is not too longer to face Generation Z learners. Generation Z is a sharing Generation. Sharing what? Later millennial and coming up Generation Z, live their lives online. They love to contribute their knowledge and option online. A statistical report points out 8% of generation Z member use twitter while 93% use YouTube to view, upload and comment on videos, they do that to feel good about themselves. As Educational scenario, is in this force, what are we Educational institutions, Teacher Educator must equip oneself to face the upcoming student teachers who are inclined towards the digital age. If learning is to have the level of quality that we dream for it, we as educators need to proactively be a part of the Blended Learning that is inevitably coming our way. Teachers must be an active part of designing online learning's rigor and quality or they will be left in the dust.

Definition of Blended Learning

Bonk and Graham in their first *Handbook of Blended Learning* defined 'Blended Learning systems' as learning systems that "combine face-to-face instruction with computer mediated instruction." Currently, use of the term Blended Learning mostly involves "combining Internet and digital media with established classroom forms that require the physical co-presence of teacher and students." Lifco dictionary states blend means, mix together different kinds of substances.

Blended Learning

The terms "blended," "hybrid," "technology-mediated instruction," "web-enhanced instruction," and "mixed-mode instruction" are often used interchangeably in current research literature.

Road of Blended Learning

Technology-based training emerged as an alternative to instructor-led training in the 1960s on mainframes and mini-computers. Mainframe-based training had a number of interface limitations that gave way to satellite-based live video in the 1970s. The advantage here was serving people who were not as PC-literate, Programmed Logic for Automatic Teaching Operations PLATO in particular had the aviation industry used this heavily to track how well one did on courses, how much time was spent, and where someone left off. AICC, Aviation Industry Computer-Based Training Committee, was formed in 1988 and companies such as Boeing used CD-ROMs to provide training for personnel. Modern Blended Learning is delivered online, although CD-ROMs could feasibly still be used if a learning management system meets an institution's standards. Some examples of channels through which online blending learning can be delivered include webcasting (synchronous and asynchronous) and online video (live and recorded). Solutions such as Khan Academy have been used in classrooms to serve as platforms for Blended Learning.

Blended Learning Equation

Face-to-Face + Synchronous Conversations + Asynchronous Interactions = Strong Online Learning Environment.

Why blend and what is being Blended?

An instructor, trainer, teacher educator or even learner must pick B.L over other learning options for many reasons like:

1. Pedagogical richness
2. Access to knowledge
3. Social interaction
4. Personal agency
5. Cost effectiveness
6. Ease of revision

We live in a world in which technological innovation is occurring at break-neck speed and digital technologies are increasingly becoming an integral part of our day-to-day lives. Therefore, it is essential to blend our learning through various pathways. The often used Blended Learning processes are listed below,

1. BL = combining instructional modalities (or delivery media).
2. BL = combining instructional methods.
3. BL = combining online and face-to-face instruction.

Blended Learning a Boon for Personalizing Education

Blended Learning is a new educational model introduced in the year 1999 but was very passive and has become vibrant in the beginning of the 21st century is of great boon to the learning community, specifically both for students and teachers. The role of teachers in Blended Learning is very prominent in improving the reasoning and creativity skill of the students. Many western schools and few schools in India use this online tool for online classes, homework, question and answer forums and other school related activities.

Merits in the implementation of Blended Learning

As the Educational field faces the millennial and generation Z learners who are hugely concerned with social political issues globally, they tend to live beyond digital age. In such atmosphere Blended Learning will serve to facilitate a simultaneous independent and collaborative learning experience and this incorporation is a major contributor to student satisfaction and success in such courses. The use of information and communication technologies has been found to improve access to as well as student attitudes towards learning. The learning has stimulated with wholehearted enthusiasm.

Demerits

Blended Learning has a strong dependence on the technical resources with which the Blended Learning experience is delivered these tools need to be reliable, easy to use, and up to date in order for the use of the Internet to have a meaningful impact on the learning experience.

Conclusion

Teacher Education = Teaching skills + Pedagogical theory + Professional Skills. Today, information is everything and it forms the part of any progressive thinking. Education today has become very effective and meaningful due to the rapid growth of technology. As a Teacher Educator one should develop and adapt to the growing technologies in order to impart knowledge to the upcoming generation. Blended Learning will serve as a platform to cater to the needs of the booming generation Z.

33

Learning Environment of the Future Students

Introduction

"An opportunity to design and build a Modern Learning Environment is an opportunity to create spaces fit for 21st century learners. As much as it's about buildings and furnishings, it's about creating spaces that promote learning that is personalised, student-centred, engaging and connected to real problems and the real world. Modern Learning Environments can help create the environment, mindsets and human capacity to help our young people make the most of their talents on the local and global stage. Students' learning needs have changed significantly. New technologies and building materials allow for new, vibrant and well connected learning spaces. All students deserve to be taught in these new modern learning environments, and benefit from new teaching methods. For faster growth of the economy of a country human capital should be available along with physical capital. That is why, improving and expanding education are essential ingredients of any national development policy. However, developing countries fail to offer education to all sections of people in society through conventional on-campus system of education due to lack of infrastructural facilities and also some constraints embodied in it.

Distance and open learning (ODL) system can play an important role to make-up this gap. In addition to allowing more students from different background, environments and geographical settings without requiring the uses of scarce on-site space, distance and open learning system also offers the educational institutions more revenue. That means, ODL system is a cost-effective way of mass education. On the other hand, especially in the developing countries, students who cannot go to school due to insolvent economic condition of the parents can have education by earning by themselves. So, ODL systems have proven themselves a way for people to gain education, which would otherwise, not possible (Dekkers, 2000). However, when comparing with conventional forms of education the provision of distance education requires considerably greater planning, larger upfront infrastructure costs and more complex student and administrative support systems (Lockwood, 1995; Rumble, 1986). Well-designed support systems facilitate the delivery of distance education courses of comparable quality and attrition rates to those for on-campus courses (NEA, 1999).

Open learning

Open learning is an innovative movement in education that emerged in the 1970s and evolved into fields of practice and study. The term refers generally to activities that either enhance learning opportunities within formal education systems or broaden learning opportunities beyond formal education systems. Open learning involves but is not limited to: classroom teaching methods, approaches to interactive learning, formats in work-related education and training, the cultures and ecologies of learning communities, and the development and use of open educational resources. While there is no agreed-upon, comprehensive definition of open learning, central focus is commonly placed on the "needs of the learner as perceived by the learner." Case studies illustrate open learning as an innovation both within and across academic disciplines, professions, social sectors and national boundaries, and in business and industry, higher education institutions, collaborative initiatives between institutions, and schooling for young learners.

Open learning as a teaching method is founded on the work of Celestin Freinet in France and Maria Montessori in Italy, among others. Open learning is supposed to allow pupils self-determined, independent and interest-guided learning. A prominent example is the language experience approach to teaching initial literacy.

E-learning

E-learning (or eLearning) is the use of electronic media and information and communication technologies (ICT) in education. E-learning is broadly inclusive of all forms of educational technology in learning and teaching. E-learning is inclusive of, and is broadly synonymous with multimedia learning, technology-enhanced learning (TEL), computer-based instruction (CBI), computer managed instruction, computer-based training (CBT), computer-assisted instruction or computer-aided instruction (CAI), internet-based training (IBT), web-based training (WBT), online education, virtual education, virtual learning environments (VLE) (which are also called learning platforms), m-learning, and digital educational collaboration. These alternative names emphasize a particular aspect, component or delivery method.

E-learning includes numerous types of media that deliver text, audio, images, animation, and streaming video, and includes technology applications and processes such as audio or video tape, satellite TV, CD-ROM, and computer-based learning, as well as local intranet/extranet and web-based learning.

E-learning can occur in or out of the classroom. It can be self-paced, asynchronous learning or may be instructor-led, synchronous learning. E-learning is suited to distance learning and flexible learning, but it can also be used in conjunction with face-to-face teaching, in which case the term blended learning is commonly used.

Open Learning through e-Learning

The advantages of Open Learning and E-Learning can be combined to provide a Learner friendly plat form. There are several advantages and disadvantages with regards to motivation in Open Learning through e-learning. For many students, e-learning is the most convenient way to pursue a degree in higher education. A lot of these students are attracted to a flexible, self-paced method of education to attain their degree. It is important to note that many of these students could be working their way through college, supporting themselves or battling with serious illness. To these students, it would be extremely difficult to find time to fit college in their schedule. Thus, these students are more likely and more motivated to enroll in an e-learning class. Moreover, in asynchronous e-learning classes, students are free to log on and complete work any time they wish. They can work on and complete their assignments at the times when they think most cogently, whether it be early in the morning or late at night.

However, many teachers have a harder time keeping their students engaged in an e-learning class. A disengaged student is usually an unmotivated student, and an engaged student is a motivated student. One reason why students are more likely to be disengaged is that the lack of face-to-face contact makes it difficult for teachers to read their students' nonverbal cues, including confusion, boredom or frustration. These cues are helpful to a teacher in deciding whether to speed up, introduce new material, slow down or explain a concept in a different way. If a student is confused, bored or frustrated, he or she is unlikely to be motivated to succeed in that class.

Conclusion

To increase the quality of Learning in Open Learning; e-learning can be adopted. This article discusses about the blended platform-Open Leaning through e-learning. The existing Distance Education Institutions should adopt e-learning methodologies in imparting Learning to their students.

References

1. http://www.core-ed.org/professional-learning/modern-learning-resources
2. Koul, B.N., Singh, Baushise; Ansari, M. M. (ed) 1988. Studies in Distance education. New Delhi, AIU.
3. IGNOU (2008). Growth and Philosophis of D.E. New Delhi, Study material of PGDDE programme
4. Harichandan, D (1999). Open University System: A broad based attempt at Distance Education. University News, V0127 No. 36 pages 3-7, New Delhi, AIU.
5. http://en.wikipedia.org/wiki/E-learning#Pedagogical_approaches

